Access your online resources

Early Years Intervention Toolkit is accompanied by a number of printable online materials, designed to ensure this resource best supports your professional needs.
   Activate your online resources:

Go to www.routledge.com/cw/speechmark and click on the cover of this book.
Click the 'Sign in or Request Access' button and follow the instructions in order to access the resources.

The Early Years Intervention Toolkit

The Early Years Intervention Toolkit provides a range of ready-made activities to enable early years practitioners and health visitors to address observed difficulties in a child's development prior to starting school.

It includes a checklist of observed behaviours which links to a range of effective and engaging activities to support children's development across the three prime foundational areas of learning: Communication and Language; Physical Development; and Personal, Social and Emotional Development. Activities focus on a variety of crucial skills such as speaking and listening, moving and handling, and forming relationships, making use of materials that are readily available in every early years setting.

This toolkit offers:

- A time-saving approach to interventions, with additional guidance on planning, providing, and recording appropriate interventions
- Advice and activities to share with parents for them to try at home
- A framework to enable early years practitioners to identify specific difficulties in key areas of development
- Downloadable resources to support activities and interventions

The Early Years Intervention Toolkit is an inclusive programme and all children in the early years will benefit from taking part in the activities. It will be an essential resource for early years practitioners to effectively identify and support learning needs in child development and will boost the confidence of young children as they prepare for Key Stage One.

Linda Tallent was for many years an early years teacher and local authority school improvement officer. She founded the Learning and Training Consultancy (LTC), a training company providing support and advice to primary schools. She worked as an independent educational consultant, providing advice, support and training locally, nationally and internationally to teachers, senior managers and local authority officers.

Her knowledge of child development and early years practice enabled her to support schools to improve the effectiveness of teaching and learning, ensuring that all children—whatever their background, gender, or special educational need—achieve as well as possible.

In her final years she continued to work tirelessly to provide EYFS practitioners with resources to help them improve their provision for children.

Jean Thompson has been a teacher for over twenty years in both Special Education and Primary mainstream schools. For the past twenty years she has been a consultant for SEND and Inclusion in a Local Authority in the North East of England. Jean has always had and continues to have a passion for promoting the early identification of and intervention for children who may require support. She now holds the additional position of Virtual School Headteacher for children in care and children in need.

Jean continues to deliver high quality training to teachers and practitioners, including those who are newly qualified . She acts as a mentor for SENDCOs from early years settings through to Secondary schools and was an associate tutor for the National Award for SENDCOs.

The Early Years Intervention Toolkit

Inclusive Activities to Support Child Development

Linda Tallent and Jean Thompson

LONDON AND NEW YORK

Cover image credit: ©Getty

First published 2022
by Routledge
2 Park Square, Milton Park, Abingdon, Oxon OX14 4RN

and by Routledge
605 Third Avenue, New York, NY 10158

Routledge is an imprint of the Taylor & Francis Group, an informa business

© 2022 Linda Tallent and Jean Thompson

The right of Linda Tallent and Jean Thompson to be identified as authors of this work has been asserted in accordance with sections 77 and 78 of the Copyright, Designs and Patents Act 1988.

All rights reserved. The purchase of this copyright material confers the right on the purchasing institution to photocopy or download pages which bear the support material icon and a copyright line at the bottom of the page. No other parts of this book may be reprinted or reproduced or utilised in any form or by any electronic, mechanical, or other means, now known or hereafter invented, including photocopying and recording, or in any information storage or retrieval system, without permission in writing from the publishers.

Trademark notice: Product or corporate names may be trademarks or registered trademarks, and are used only for identification and explanation without intent to infringe.

British Library Cataloguing-in-Publication Data
A catalogue record for this book is available from the British Library

Library of Congress Cataloging-in-Publication Data
Names: Tallent, Linda, author. | Thompson, Jean, 1958– author.
Title: The early years intervention toolkit : inclusive activities to
   support child development / Linda Tallent and Jean Thompson.
Description: Abingdon, Oxon ; New York, NY : Routledge, 2022. |
   Includes index.
Identifiers: LCCN 2021034239 (print) | LCCN 2021034240 (ebook) |
   ISBN 9781032152561 (hardback) | ISBN 9781032152547 (paperback) |
   ISBN 9781003243298 (ebook)
Subjects: LCSH: Child development. | Early childhood
   education—Psychological aspects. | Children—Language. |
   Children—Communication. | Emotions in children. | Social skills in
   children.
Classification: LCC LB1115 .T145 2022 (print) | LCC LB1115 (ebook) |
   DDC 372.21—dc23
LC record available at https://lccn.loc.gov/2021034239
LC ebook record available at https://lccn.loc.gov/2021034240

ISBN: 978-1-032-15256-1 (hbk)
ISBN: 978-1-032-15254-7 (pbk)
ISBN: 978-1-003-24329-8 (ebk)

DOI: 10.4324/9781003243298

Typeset in Univers
by Apex CoVantage, LLC

Access the companion website: www.routledge.com/cw/speechmark

Contents

Chapter 1 The importance of early identification and intervention   1

Chapter 2 Making meaningful observations   4

Chapter 3 Using the Early Years Intervention Toolkit   8

Chapter 4 Checklists of observed behaviours   12

Chapter 5 The early years intervention activities   18

Chapter 6 Parents as partners   63

Chapter 7 Parent support activities (PSA)   67

Index   *100*

1 The importance of early identification and intervention

The importance of early identification—the recognition of possible delays in reaching early milestones or differences in behaviour or development—and intervention, especially in the first five years of life, has been emphasised for many years and continues to be a focus in the Early Years. The benefits of early identification and intervention can help prevent further problems developing in the future as the child continues along their journey through education and life and can reduce the need for costly interventions and greatly benefit parents in supporting their young children.

Children often arrive at their first learning and education provision without the key skills they need to learn and progress well. There may be elements of their development that are delayed or they may have gaps in their development for a number of reasons. Being behind in development in the early years of life can have a significant impact on the child achieving their full potential and may develop significant barriers to learning. It can also cause the child to present a range of different behaviours, which are often the first things that we notice. These can often be addressed simply as behavioural issues without finding the underlying cause.

Children wake each day with the wonderment of what lies ahead. They want to have fun, positive experiences and interactions with children and adults and they naturally want to please. They do not wake up and plan to "not do the right thing". However, as we all know, many children struggle to do these "right things" and can often present behaviours that we may not expect or like.

If we notice differences in behaviour early, there will always be a reason for it and it may be linked to an area of development that may need intervention. These differences in behaviour might present as:

- Refusal to comply (not following instructions)
- Disrupting others/poor social interaction
- Hiding or being withdrawn
- Running away/avoiding people/tasks
- Hitting out, biting, showing aggression
- Following their own agenda
- Tiredness
- Emotional, angry, crying, generally unhappy

When helping practitioners to identify a cause for concern, we ask them to think about the behaviour the child is presenting and say, "*If only they could or if only they would . . ., what would that be?*". Some examples of responses were, "*If only they*

2 The importance of early identification and intervention

could sit still on the carpet", "If only they wouldn't snatch toys", "If only they would follow my instructions" or *"If only they would engage with other children".*

The responses to the question have already identified a barrier to successful learning. The next step is to ask *"WHY"* this behaviour is happening and begin to investigate through observations, discussions with parents and staff and identifying possible triggers. We can then implement an appropriate intervention. If we only look at and consider the *behaviour* and attempt to support this without looking at the cause, we will be much less successful in helping the child to move forward in their development. In many cases it can have the opposite effect and cause increased frustration in the child.

Behaviours that are different from what we expect are always the result of something else, they are not planned by the young child. We need to identify what this "something else" is and provide systematic interventions to address the issues and help the children to become successful learners.

Systematic early intervention is the key to giving these children the foundations they need to reach their potential and to become lifelong learners.

The 2014 SEND Code of Practice (which is just as valid today as it was then) puts emphasis on the importance of early identification and schools' role within this:

All schools should have a clear approach to identifying and responding to SEN. The benefits of early identification are widely recognised – identifying need at the earliest point and then making effective provision to improve long-term outcomes for the child or young person.

(Section 6.14 of the Code)

If a child is identified as having a gap or being behind in their development, this does not necessarily mean that they will have a Special Educational Need. However, early identification and intervention can identify a specific need early and with the appropriate early intervention can significantly improve the life chances of those who do have a Special Educational Need.

If every child is to be given the chance to become a successful learner, schools and settings need to identify from the very beginning children who are not attaining age-related expectations in Communication and Language, in Physical Development and in Personal, Social and Emotional Development. Effective intervention in the early years can reduce the gap and improve outcomes for those children who are working below age-related expectations.

Interventions that produce positive outcomes for children are those that meet the individual needs of the child. In order to determine the specific needs of a child who is at risk of not meeting their potential, practitioners should interact with the child and observe them taking part in child-initiated activities. Discussion with parents and carers will give the practitioner insight into the family situation. This information can then be used to plan challenging and appropriate activities that will be tailored to the individual needs of the child. Once an intervention programme is in place, practitioners need to track the child's progress and measure the impact of the programme.

In order for intervention to be successful, practitioners have a crucial role in supporting the child to reach their full potential. Engaging with the child in systematically

The importance of early identification and intervention

planned, multi-sensory, play-based activities that address their area of need will enable the child to move beyond their current limits.

What can we reasonably expect from young children? As adults our social relationships are built on give and take, making allowances, consideration of feelings, circumstances and individual needs, mutual respect, valuing the individual. All of this applies to our relationships with children and our expectations of them. Therefore, our expectations of children must be realistic and take account of their age, stage of development and emotional state.

2 Making meaningful observations

Making the time to closely observe and listen to children is the most effective way of identifying delays in development and differences in behaviour. It is a privilege to be able to watch how children communicate, interact and behave with their peers and adults and how they physically move around an environment.

When children arrive in a school or a setting for the first time, the experienced teacher or practitioner will immediately spot anything "different". The first thing to note is often a child's behaviour, whether it is unusual, undesirable or simply different to that of their peers.

It is appropriate to allow a short period of time for a child to adjust to a new environment, teacher or group of friends. In the Early Years, a child who is coming into a setting for the very first time and leaving Mum, Dad, Gran or carer, can be very daunted and become anxious. Once that period of settling has passed, if your concerns about the child's development or behaviour remain, then close observations are necessary. Consider the child in a completely holistic way. Avoid focusing on what you *think* might be an issue.

Behaviour is often the first thing that alerts us to a delay or difference and this can often be a barrier to successful learning. Our main aim is to identify what this barrier might be and try to remove it or reduce it.

Ask yourself "*If only he would . . .*" or "*If only she could. . . .*".

For example, "*If only Tommy could take turns . . .*" or "*If only Sophie would stop pulling hair . . .*". You are already identifying a barrier that is preventing the child from learning successfully. This can be applied to any child in any primary key stage.

Creating an holistic profile

In order to create an holistic profile for a child and to find out where there may be a delay or a barrier to learning, we must observe the child. We should be focusing on the child's behaviour for learning and it is essential that we consider all aspects of development and cover the prime areas of development and learning:

- Speech, Language and Communication
- Physical development
- Emotional, Social and Mental Health and Cognitive development

If you create a profile for a child, based on observational assessment, you will need to consider all areas of development:

DOI: 10.4324/9781003243298-2

Making meaningful observations 5

Holistic Profile Checklist	
Speech, Language and Communication	Note your observations here. Describe what you see or hear
• **Speech** (articulation, clarity and fluency)	***Concern:*** *e.g. speech unclear. Initial and final sounds replaced in several words, e.g. "gog" for dog, "tar" for car.* ***No concern:*** *e.g. has age-appropriate language and can easily be understood.*
• **Receptive language** (understanding of instructions—how do you know the child understands you?)	***Concern:*** *e.g. doesn't do as asked. Often copies other children. Sometimes does the wrong thing.* ***No concern:*** *e.g. always follows instructions on the first time of asking. Picks up new concepts easily.*
• **Language processing** (does the child take more time than expected time to respond?)	
• **Expressive language** (word finding, word ordering, sentence structure, etc.)	
• **Communication** (willingness, verbal, non-verbal)	
Social Interaction	Note your observations here. Describe what you see or hear.
• **Friendships**	
• **Cooperation** (sharing, turn taking, etc.)	
• **Appropriateness** (is the child socially aware?)	
• **Desire** (does the child want to play or be with others?)	
Attention, Listening and Memory	Note your observations here. Describe what you see or hear.
• **Sitting** (for how long and the behaviour displayed)	
• **Looking and listening** (calmness, eye contact, distracted, etc.)	
• **Completion of tasks** (distracted, unfinished activities, flitting)	
• **Task focus** (ability to stay on task)	
• **Auditory memory** (retention of verbal information)	
• **Visual memory** (retention of visual information)	

Copyright material from [Tallent and Thompson (2022), *The Early Years Intervention Toolkit*, Routledge]

6   Making meaningful observations

Planning and Organisation	Note your observations here. Describe what you see or hear.
• **Personal organisation** (ability to independently organise themselves)	
• **Making choices** (can the child decide what to do without help?)	
• **Self-help skills** (dressing, toileting, eating, etc.)	
Motor Skills and Movement	Note your observations here. Describe what you see or hear.
• **Fine motor skills** (pencil grip, writing skills, dressing)	
• **Gross motor skills** (walking, running, climbing, etc.)	
• **Spatial awareness** (tripping, falling, bumping into things, etc.)	
• **Ability to sit still** (keeping their body still, controlling movement)	
Behaviour	Note your observations here. Describe what you see or hear.
• In the classroom	
• Outdoors	
• Other areas	
• At home	
Strengths	Note your observations here. Describe what you see or hear.
• Social	
• Learning	
• Interests	
• Other skills	
Barrier(s) to learning identified	
Interventions to try	

Copyright material from [Tallent and Thompson (2022), *The Early Years Intervention Toolkit*, Routledge]

By completing these observations, you will form an holistic and meaningful assessment of the child. It may confirm your first thoughts but also guide you towards something that you may not have considered. Any challenging or unexpected behaviour that the child may be presenting can then often be explained and therefore managed more successfully. Systematic interventions can then be tailored to meet the child's needs, ensuring successful outcomes.

Only if these systematic, daily interventions fail to improve the development of the child and the barriers to learning, would the next level of interventions be required, i.e. further assessment.

3 | Using the Early Years Intervention Toolkit

The Early Years Intervention Toolkit is a programme of activities that will support practitioners to meet the needs of those children who are not meeting age-related expectations in their Communication and Language, Physical, and Personal, Social and Emotional Development. The purpose of the programme is to improve children's development across these three areas, which are the foundations to learning.

The Early Years Intervention Toolkit is an ***inclusive*** programme, and all children in the Early Years will benefit from taking part in the activities. The suggested activities should be delivered as part of the broad, balanced curriculum that all children within the school or setting access.

The role of the practitioner (or indeed any member of staff or adult helper) is to support and scaffold a child's learning and development. Critical to this role is the need to develop respectful relationships with both children and parents. By listening to and valuing what parents tell them about their children, practitioners can form a complete picture of the child. Through observing and interacting sensitively and responsively to children, practitioners are able to assess children's learning needs and use the Early Years Intervention Toolkit to plan and provide appropriate interventions. The Intervention Record Sheet can be used to evidence progress.

Using the Early Years Intervention Toolkit

In order to identify a behaviour or difficulty, practitioners should have observed the child consistently over time. Following your observations of the child and discussions with other staff members and parents, you make a note of the behaviours and/or difficulties you have observed. These could be in one or more areas of development. You need to consider which behaviour is the main barrier to the child fulfilling their potential. Having done this, practitioners can then move on to the Checklists of Observed Behaviours.

These checklists will help to develop a plan of specific interventions that will support the child to overcome barriers to learning. The Checklists of Observed Behaviours consist of statements that describe behaviours or difficulties you may have observed. If these behaviours and difficulties are not addressed they may become a barrier to learning.

There is a Checklist of Observed Behaviours for each of the three areas of development that are the foundations for all learning:

- Communication and language
  - Speaking and Expression
  - Listening and Attention
  - Supporting Receptive Language and Communication
- Physical development
  - Moving and Handling
  - Health and Self-care
- Personal, social and emotional development
  - Making Relationships
  - Self-confidence and Self-awareness
  - Managing Feelings and Behaviours

Using the checklists of observed behaviours

An example of a checklist of observed behaviours

PHYSICAL DEVELOPMENT	
Movement is a fundamental activity of life. Balance and coordination are essential for successful learning. Limited early movement experiences or an inborn condition such as Developmental Coordination Disorder can cause delay in physical movement. Therefore, early identification and intervention is vital to support children who enter nursery below age related expectations.	
MOVING AND HANDLING	
OBSERVED BEHAVIOUR	Intervention Activity
• Walks awkwardly or frequently trips.	18, 19, 20

The practitioner observes that the child "walks awkwardly". The intervention programme to support the observed behaviour begins with Intervention Activity 18. The practitioner begins by carrying out the activities on Activity 18 and then progresses through the next activities in numerical order.

The Intervention Activities

The Intervention Activities provide the practitioner with activities and strategies that will support and extend the child's learning. They focus on developing specific skills and provide assessment advice.

Most of the suggested activities and strategies can take place in both the indoor or outdoor environments. It is recognised that some children prefer working in the outdoor environment. Working outdoors provides different experiences and, in some cases, triggers differences in children's behaviour. The Intervention Activities will support practitioners to deliver personalised learning to help children get the best start in life.

Using the Early Years Intervention Toolkit

For many of the Intervention Activity Sheets, Parental Support Activity Sheets (PSAs) have also been provided. These activity sheets have been designed to be used in the home by parents, carers or any adults wishing to support the work done by practitioners. These can be copied and given to the adult along with explanations on how to carry out the activities. Bear in mind that for many adults, following the printed instructions may be daunting and it may be preferable to give them simplified, verbal directions. The important thing to remember is that the activities should be fun! Picture cards to accompany some of the activities (Letter Sounds, Objects and Activities) can be downloaded and printed out to be sent home.

Intervention Record Sheet

After each intervention session the practitioner uses the Intervention Record Sheet to document which Intervention Activity has been followed and which step on the activity sheet that the child is working on. The record can either be made on a printed sheet or made electronically using a template downloaded onto an electronic device.

An example of a completed Intervention Record Sheet

Intervention Record Sheet					
Child's Name: **Sam Wilson**					
Observed Behaviour: Walks awkwardly or frequently trips.			Focus: To improve balance and stability.		
Intervention number: 18					
Step/Activity	Date	Comments	Attitude indicators	Progress indicators	Next Steps
1	5/10	Was hesitant to walk between lines—needed to hold my hand. Wobbled. Right foot wandered over line. Found it funny. Enjoyed the activity.	E	SD V-SamW1	Repeat and possibly widen gap between tapes Step 2

Attitude indicators:
  P – participated fully   **E** – engaged   **D** – disengaged

Progress indicators:
  SI – Significant improvement in achieving the skill   **D** – Developing the skill
  SD – Significant difficulty in achieving the skill difficulty

Evidence:
  PH – photograph   **V** – video

The Intervention Record provides practitioners with a systematic method for recording interventions and monitoring the progress of individual children. If the child continues to have significant difficulty in achieving a particular skill and evidence indicates they are making insufficient or no progress after four weeks of intervention, you should consider consulting the school/setting SENDco or inclusion manager.

Using the Early Years Intervention Toolkit

Intervention Record Sheet						
Child's Name:							
Observed Behaviour:				Focus:		
Intervention Activity number:							
Step/Activity	Date	Comments	Attitude Indicators	Progress Indicators	Next Steps

Attitude indicators:
  P – participated fully   **E** – engaged   **D** – disengaged

Progress indicators:
  SI – Significant improvement in achieving the skill   **D** – Developing the skill
  SD – Significant difficulty in achieving the skill difficulty

Evidence:
  PH –photograph   **V** – video

Copyright material from [Tallent and Thompson (2022), *The Early Years Intervention Toolkit*, Routledge]

4 | Checklists of observed behaviours

COMMUNICATION and LANGUAGE
SPEAKING

Some children may be reluctant to speak for a number of reasons. It may be because English is not their first language or because the child is electing not to speak. This is more common in young children, perhaps in the first weeks of starting school.

Reluctant speakers will go through a period of silence. The transition from silence to speech will depend on how this is managed by the teacher and the child. These children should not be considered for any specific interventions.

*These indicators may be linked to an early or current hearing difficulty. A referral to a GP and/or Speech and Language Therapist might be considered.

"Glue ear" is extremely common in young children. Children who are prone to frequent ear infections or a runny nose may experience intermittent hearing loss. This can fluctuate from day to day and can significantly affect a child's ability to accurately hear and copy sounds in speech.

SPEAKING

OBSERVED BEHAVIOUR	Intervention Activity
Very limited or no speech.	1
Unintelligible speech.	1
Immature speech.	2
Poor articulation of phonemes and words.*	3
Omission of initial and final phonemes.*	3
Substitution of phonemes (initial, medial or final, or omission).*	3
Slurred speech.	4
Salivates excessively.	4
Reluctance or continuing refusal to speak.	5
Dysfluency (stammer).	5

DOI: 10.4324/9781003243298-4

Checklists of observed behaviours

EXPRESSION	
OBSERVED BEHAVIOUR	**Intervention Activity**
Unable to put two words or more together (age-related expectation at 24 months).	6
Have difficulty finding the right words.	7
Unable to use "I", "me" and "my" correctly.	8
Mis-names objects.	7
Unable to hold a simple conversation (age-related expectation at 36 months).	9
Unable to convey thoughts and ideas coherently.	9
May not appear to hear or listen.	10
Doesn't respond to greetings.	10
Looks at the speaker, but shows little or no response.	11
Shifts attention from one thing to another.	12
Compared to their peers, they are unable to maintain attention.	11
May be quiet and withdrawn.	15
May talk continually and doesn't appear to understand the rules of conversation.	14
Inability to sit still, fidgets, is easily distracted.	13
Only able to concentrate for very short periods of time.	11
Fleeting eye contact.	10
Presents attention and listening difficulties.	11
Plays in isolation.	15

14 Checklists of observed behaviours

COMMUNICATION and LANGUAGE
Supporting Receptive Language and Communication

This is an aspect of speech, language and communication that can often be overlooked as children may often appear to ignore verbal instructions and follow their own agenda. Children develop their own strategies to overcome their lack of understanding spoken language. Children may demonstrate some or all of the indicators below. These activities will provide practitioners with strategies to address a delay in receptive language.

This is an area that practitioners can support within the learning environment. If interventions do not improve the receptive language delay, then they may require Speech and Language therapy.

UNDERSTANDING

OBSERVED BEHAVIOUR	Intervention Activity
Doesn't respond to simple verbal instructions.	16, 17
Requires a high level of non-verbal communication e.g. gesturing, visual clues, signing.	16, 17
Often repeats the last word of a sentence or a whole phrase.	16, 17
Unable to identify an object by name.	16, 17
May watch and copy other children.	16, 17
Frequently looks for visual cues.	16, 17
When asked a question, gives an inappropriate "yes or no" answer.	16, 17
Finds learning new concepts difficult.	16, 17
Is unable to understand prepositions.	16, 17
Unable to understand why, where, what, when and how questions.	16, 17
Presents attention and listening difficulties.	16, 17
Unable to join in with whole/small group activities.	16, 17

Checklists of observed behaviours 15

PHYSICAL DEVELOPMENT

Movement is a fundamental activity of life. Balance and coordination are essential for successful learning. Limited early movement experiences or an inborn condition such as Developmental Coordination Disorder can cause delay in physical movement. Therefore early identification and intervention is vital to support children who enter nursery below age-related expectations.

MOVING AND HANDLING

OBSERVED BEHAVIOUR	Intervention Activity
Walks awkwardly or frequently trips.	18, 19, 20
Prefers to run rather than walk.	18, 19, 20
Often bumps into things.	21
Has difficulty negotiating space or demonstrates poor spatial awareness.	21
Difficulty with pedalling a tricycle or similar toy.	22
Prefers to lie rather than sit on the carpet.	23
Unable to sustain an upright sitting position.	23
Has difficulty in getting from a sitting position to a standing position.	23
Finds climbing up and down stairs difficult.	18, 19, 20, 23
Unable to jump with two feet, hop on one leg or balance on one foot (age-related expectation at 50 months).	18, 19, 20
Unable to hold a pencil between thumb and finger and make controlled marks (age-related expectation at 50 months).	24
Shows difficulties in cutting (age-related expectation at 50 months).	25
Shows difficulties in threading (age-related expectation at 50 months).	25
Avoidance of small constructional toys, such as jigsaws or building blocks.	26

Checklists of observed behaviours

HEALTH AND SELF CARE	
OBSERVED BEHAVIOUR	**Intervention Activity**
Continued messy eating—struggles to eat with cutlery.	27
May prefer to eat with their fingers.	27
Struggles with dressing.	28
Excessive salivation.	29

Personal Social and Emotional Development
Making Relationships

Personal, Social and Emotional development are the three building blocks of life. Children need to have a sense of who they are, how to form relationships and understand and manage their feelings and emotions if they are to become lifelong learners.

MAKING RELATIONSHIPS	
OBSERVED BEHAVIOUR	**Intervention Activity**
Shows no desire to play alongside others (age-related expectation at 36 months).	30
Shows little or no concern for other children's feelings or demonstrates an inappropriate response.	31
Doesn't interact with other children.	32
Inability to share and turn-take with other children.	33, 34
Demonstrates little self-control of own behaviour in conflict situations.	35
Finds it difficult to form good relationships with children and/or adults.	36

Checklists of observed behaviours 17

Children need to be confident to try new things and say why they like some activities more than others. They should be confident enough to speak in a familiar group and talk about their ideas. They should be able to select their resources and say whether they need help or not.

SELF CONFIDENCE and SELF AWARENESS

OBSERVED BEHAVIOUR	Intervention Activity
Has continued difficulty separating from parent or carer.	37
Appears quiet, withdrawn and nervous.	38
Lacks confidence in speaking to adults and/or other children.	39
Needs support to encouragement to select activities independently.	40
Has predictable routines, always plays in the same areas, is reluctant to try new activities or "have a go" with different resources.	41

Children need to have an awareness of their actions and realise that what they do may hurt others. Turn taking and the sharing of resources is important. Children should learn to talk about how they feel and learn that some behaviour is unacceptable and accept that some behaviours may have consequences.

MANAGING FEELINGS AND BEHAVIOUR

OBSERVED BEHAVIOUR	Intervention Activity
Is unaware of the consequences of their own behaviour.	42, 43
Responds inappropriately when others are upset or hurt.	44
Is unable to show an understanding of their emotions.	44
Finds difficulty in adapting their behaviour in different situations.	42, 43
Shows a lack of awareness of the boundaries and expectations within the setting.	42, 43
Has difficulty in coping with "change".	42, 43

5 | The early years intervention activities

Communication and language
Speaking

		Card 1
The activities below are graded according to difficulty. Begin with the activity described in Step 1. Move on to the next step only when the child shows confidence and success. You may find that the child progresses through the first steps quickly. It is important to provide opportunities for the child to practice the activities daily.		

Observed behaviour	• Very limited or no speech. • Unintelligible speech.
Focus	• To develop two way non-verbal communication.
Activity/ Strategy	To develop the child's nonverbal communication with both adults and peers. **Step 1** The adult introduces the concept of picture exchange. To begin, the adult provides five single-word object picture cards and five matching objects, which relate to the child's interests. Model picture object exchange with another adult, e.g. one adult chooses a picture of a spade, the other adult finds the spade and they exchange card and spade. The adult repeats this several times using different objects. The adult then encourages the child to choose a picture card, show it to the adult who then provides the child with their chosen object. This activity is to be repeated daily until the child is confident in exchanging a picture for an object. **Step 2** The adult introduces five activity picture cards. The adult encourages the child to select an activity picture card and show it to the adult. The adult goes to or carries out the activity with the child. **Step 3** Provide all adults with duplicate copies of picture prompts to use when communicating with the child. Simple visual hand gestures can be introduced to support the conveyance of meaning (Makaton signs or something similar). **Step 4** Increase and vary the word/picture cards linked to the child's preferences and interests. Provide all adults with a lanyard holding a wide range of object and activity cards to use when communicating with the child. ***Refer to speech and language therapy***
Assessment	• Observe the child's communication skills both before the intervention and after. • Use the Intervention Record Sheet to record evidence of progress.
Outcome	• The child will be able to communicate with both adults and peers more successfully and confidently.
Resources	• Object and activity picture cards. • Lanyard. • Makaton symbols. • PSA Card 1. • Intervention Record Sheet.
If the child continues to have significant difficulty in achieving a particular skill and evidence indicates they are making insufficient or no progress after four weeks of intervention you should consider consulting the school or setting SENDco.	

DOI: 10.4324/9781003243298-5

The early years intervention activities | **19**

Communication and language
Speaking

The activities below are graded according to difficulty. Begin with the activity described in Step 1. Move on to the next step only when the child shows confidence and success. You may find that the child progresses through the first steps quickly. It is important to provide opportunities for the child to practice the activities daily.		**Card 2**

Observed behaviour	• Immature speech. For example, "*Can me put baba in cot*" instead of, "*Can I put the baby in the cot*" or "*Her sitting on chair*" instead of "*She is sitting on the chair*".
Focus	• To develop age appropriate expressive language.
Activity/ Strategy	To develop sentence structure from single words. **Step 1** The adult sits with the child for five minutes each day and presents a range of single object picture cards. The adult models the correct pronunciation of the words and asks the child to repeat the words. **Step 2** The adult intervenes regularly in the child's play and models the correct sentence structure where appropriate. **Step 3** The adult shares a picture book and randomly asks the child a question, e.g. "*What is Emily doing?*". The adult repeats the child's answer and extends it if necessary.
Assessment	• Observe the development of the child's expressive language. • If there is none or little improvement, you should request a hearing assessment. Consider referring to speech and language therapy.
Outcome	• The child is able to use age-appropriate sounds, words and sentences.
Resources	• Single-object picture cards. • Picture book. • Intervention Record Sheet.

If the child continues to have significant difficulty in achieving a particular skill and evidence indicates they are making insufficient or no progress after four weeks of intervention you should consider consulting the school or setting SENDco.

The early years intervention activities

Communication and language
Speaking

The activities below are graded according to difficulty. Begin with the activity described in Step 1. Move on to the next step only when the child shows confidence and success. You may find that the child progresses through the first steps quickly. It is important to provide opportunities for the child to practice the activities daily.		**Card 3**

Observed behaviour	• Poor articulation of phonemes and words. • Omission of initial and final phonemes. • Substitution or omission of initial, medial or final phonemes.
Focus	• To develop the child's pronunciation of sounds and words.
Activity/ Strategy	***Note: this may be directly linked to a conductive hearing loss therefore the child should be referred for a hearing assessment.*** **Step 1** The adult and the child should sit outside the classroom for this intervention in order to reduce background noise. The child may have difficulty identifying particular frequencies. The adult assesses the child's pronunciation of a range of sounds using picture cards. The adult notes the inaccuracies. **Step 2** The adult must first identify the consistent irregularities. The adult then demonstrates to the child the shape of the mouth for each different sound selected. The adult uses actions to demonstrate the sound such as "*Mmmm*" and rub the tummy. The adult gives the child a mirror so that they can compare the shape of their mouth with yours. Some sounds are formed in the back of the mouth and these are more difficult to model and explain so begin with those where the mouth shape is more easily modelled. **Step 3** The adult repeats Step 2 on a daily basis then moves into the classroom. The adult repeats Step 2 again within a more noisy environment.
Assessment	• Listen to the improvement in the child's sound production. • Use the Intervention Record Sheet to record evidence of progress.
Outcome	• The child will be able to produce more clearly articulated sounds and use them appropriately in words.
Resources	• Picture or sound cards. • Mirror. • PSA Card 2. • Intervention Record Sheet.
If the child continues to have significant difficulty in achieving a particular skill and evidence indicates they are making insufficient or no progress after four weeks of intervention you should consider consulting the school or setting SENDco.	

The early years intervention activities 21

Communication and language
Speaking

		Card 4
The activities below are graded according to difficulty. Begin with the activity described in Step 1. Move on to the next step only when the child shows confidence and success. You may find that the child progresses through the first steps quickly. It is important to provide opportunities for the child to practice the activities daily.		

Observed behaviour	• Slurred speech. • Salivates excessively.
Focus	• To improve the clarity of sounds and words.
Activity/ Strategy	To exercise and tighten muscles in the mouth in order to produce clear sharp sounds and words by blowing, sucking and licking. **Step 1** The adult and child play a game of picture object snap. Encourage the child to say the name of each picture as they play the game. The adult identifies the sounds and/or words with which the child has difficulty. These should be used as a baseline. **Step 2** The adult provides daily opportunities for muscle exercise: • **Blowfish.** Cut out paper fish to blow along the floor. Use a large space such as the hall. Child has to crawl along and blow the fish from one end to the other. • **Blow football.** Provide a TUF spot (builder's tray). Place goals at the opposite sides of the tray. Ask the child and a partner to blow a ping pong ball from one side to the other and try to score a goal. Mark the tray, colour the balls, etc. to make it look like a game of football. • **Blow painting.** • **Blowing bubbles.** • **Suck it up.** Ask the child to transfer paper shapes from one tray to another using a straw to suck and hold the paper. • **Lick and stick.** Make a collage with gummed paper. Lots of licking!!! • **Honey lips.** Spread honey on the child's lips then ask the child to lick them clean. • **Cheeky cheeks.** Ask the child to blow their cheeks out. Show them how to move the air from cheek to cheek. • **Funny face.** Ask the child to pull a funny face whilst looking in a mirror and hold it for five seconds, building up to ten seconds. **The challenge** • How long can the child hold a ping pong ball on the end of a tube by sucking? • How long can they hold a funny face?
Assessment	• Play picture object snap. Listen for improved clarity of the sounds and words. • Use the Intervention Record Sheet to record evidence of progress.
Outcome	• The child will produce sharper, clearer sounds and words. • Salivation will be reduced.
Resources	• Paper fish. • TUF spot. • Straws. • Ping pong balls. • Goals. • Gummed paper. • Honey. • Mirror. • PSA Card 10. • Intervention Record Sheet.

If the child continues to have significant difficulty in achieving a particular skill and evidence indicates they are making insufficient or no progress after four weeks of intervention you should consider consulting the school or setting SENDco.

22 The early years intervention activities

Communication and language
Speaking

		Card 5
The following guidance is based on strategies rather than activities. It is important to remember what **NOT** to do as well as what to do. Too much focus and pressure may make the dysfunction worse.		

Observed behaviour	• Reluctant to speak. • Dysfluency.
Focus	• To improve the child's confidence in talking.
Activity/ Strategy	**Always:** • Allow time. Wait patiently for the child to respond. If the child is struggling, ask them to show you by pointing to an object, activity or picture card or draw what the child is trying to communicate. • Value everything the child says even if they don't finish it. • Repeat and model what the child is trying to express. **Never:** • Rush the child or show impatience. • Ask the child to take a deep breath or slow down. • Finish their sentences for them. • Ask them to think about what they want to say. • Ask them to start again. **Activities** • Singing. Dysfluent children can often sing fluently so provide plenty of opportunities for them to sing. • Try singing your request and ask them to sing their response. Do this only if the child has the confidence to do it.
Assessment	• Observe the child, note their behaviour around talking, both to their peers and to adults. • Use the Intervention Record Sheet to record evidence of progress.
Outcome	• The child will develop more confidence in talking and make more attempts at speaking to adults and peers. Disfluency will reduce. • **Note:** parents and other members of the family must be advised to follow the same advice at home.
Resources	• Intervention Record Sheet.

If the child continues to have significant difficulty in achieving a particular skill and evidence indicates they are making insufficient or no progress after four weeks of intervention you should consider consulting the school or setting SENDco.

The early years intervention activities   **23**

Communication and language
Expression

The activities below are graded according to difficulty. Begin with the activity described in Step 1. Move on to the next step only when the child shows confidence and success. You may find that the child progresses through the first steps quickly. It is important to provide opportunities for the child to practice the activities daily.		**Card 6**

Observed behaviour	• Unable to put two words together (age-related expectation at 24 months). If a child is not able to do this it may indicate a significant delay. Referral to a speech and language therapist may be considered.
Focus	• To develop the child's ability to construct and say simple sentences.
Activity/ Strategy	To develop two-word phrases. This requires regular targeted one-to-one support. **Step 1** The adult shows the child a range of activity "action" cards. The adult models the simple two-word phrase as the cards are shown to the child, e.g. *Mummy . . . jump, man . . . dig, dog . . . run.* Don't expect a response to begin with. The adult repeats the activity for five minutes daily until the child begins to repeat the short phrase. Indicate to the child that it is **two** words you are wanting by holding two fingers up. **Step 2** The adult introduces a wider range of vocabulary to develop two-word noun/action phrases. Use finger prompts for two words. **Step 3** Transfer this strategy into the everyday play situation. The adult models a sentence with two key words, stressing the noun and action, e.g. *"Can you push the car?".* **The challenge** The adult adds the child's name to a short phrase, e.g. *"Bobby digs in the sand".* The adult models this consistently until the child eventually repeats the extended phrase.
Assessment	• Observe the child using two-word phrases. Praise and reward for success. • Use the Intervention Record Sheet to record evidence of progress.
Outcome	• The child will be beginning to develop two/three-word phrases and use them spontaneously when speaking.
Resources	• Action cards. • Intervention Record Sheet.

If the child continues to have significant difficulty in achieving a particular skill and evidence indicates they are making insufficient or no progress after four weeks of intervention you should consider consulting the school or setting SENDco.

24 The early years intervention activities

Communication and language
Expression

		Card 7
The activities below are graded according to difficulty. Begin with the activity described in Step 1. Move on to the next step only when the child shows confidence and success. You may find that the child progresses through the first steps quickly. It is important to provide opportunities for the child to practice the activities daily.		

Observed behaviour	- Has difficulty finding the correct words. - Misnames objects.
Focus	- To develop single-word vocabulary.
Activity/ Strategy	To learn and use an extended range of new vocabulary. **Step 1** The adult shows the child a selection of object picture cards or real objects. The adult and child name the objects together. After three sessions, the adult sets aside the objects the child knows confidently. **Step 2** The adult and child work together to learn the names of objects. The adult groups the cards together in categories, e.g. fruit, toys, clothing, transport, furniture, etc. Begin with five objects in each group. Play the following games: **Speedy naming game:** The adult shows the child a card, the child says what it is as quickly as they can. **What's missing?:** The adult lays the cards selected from one of the groups on the table. The adult removes one card while the child is not looking and the child is asked to say which one is missing. The games should be repeated with all the groups of cards. **Step 3** The adult asks the child to think of more objects to add to each group. **The challenge** The adult begins a sentence, e.g. *"You sit on a. . . ."* . *" You peel an. . ."* *"You drive a. . ."*. The child completes the sentence. Of course there could be several answers to a question.
Assessment	- Check how many objects the child can recall and name. Can they complete sentences correctly? - Use the Intervention Record Sheet to record evidence of progress.
Outcome	- The child will now have an extended range of vocabulary, will name them correctly and find the correct word to use more easily.
Resources	- Object picture cards. - Range of real objects. - Intervention Record Sheet.

If the child continues to have significant difficulty in achieving a particular skill and evidence indicates they are making insufficient or no progress after four weeks of intervention you should consider consulting the school or setting SENDco.

Communication and language
Expression

The activities below are graded according to difficulty. Begin with the activity described in Step 1. Move on to the next step only when the child shows confidence and success. You may find that the child progresses through the first steps quickly. It is important to provide opportunities for the child to practice the activities daily.		**Card 8**

Observed behaviour	• Unable to use "*I*", "*me*" and "*my*" correctly, e.g. "*Me want . . .*", "*My have . . .*" or "*Can Jason have. . .*".
Focus	• To reduce the confusion of *me*, *my* and *I*. • To teach the child when and how to use the "target" words in the correct context.
Activity/ Strategy	To encourage and teach the child to say, for example, "*I want. . . .*", "*I have . . .*", "*I will . . .*" etc. "*Can I . . .*", "*May I . . .*", "*Could I. . .*". etc. Or "*This belongs to me*". **Step 1** The adult sits with the child. The adult selects a range of familiar objects and lays them on a table. The adult models "*I want*" or "*I would like an. . .*". then selects the object. The adult repeats this once more with a different object. The child is then encouraged to copy. If they say "*me want*" or "*Jason wants*", model the correct use of "*I*". The adult and child repeat this activity with a wider range of objects. The adult repeats the activity with the child using "*I can*" and "*I have*". **Step 2** The adult introduces "*I will*" to the child and models an action word, e.g. "*I will jump*" (the adult actually jumps). "*I will run*" (the adult actually runs). The adult asks the child to choose an action and tells you what they are doing. The activity is to be repeated using "*I am . . .*". **Step 3** The adult selects a range of objects and shares them between the adult and child. The adult selects one object and says, "*This belongs to me*". The adult encourages the child to do the same. Repeat this activity until the child is secure with using "*me*". **The challenge** When appropriate, the adult extends the sentence and models "*This car belongs to me, it is **mine***".
Assessment	• Observe the child in play. Listen to their interaction with peers and adults. • Use the Intervention Record Sheet to record evidence of progress.
Outcome	• The child will use "*I*", "*me*" and "*my*" correctly.
Resources	• Objects and picture cards. • Intervention Record Sheet.

If the child continues to have significant difficulty in achieving a particular skill and evidence indicates they are making insufficient or no progress after four weeks of intervention you should consider consulting the school or setting SENDco.

The early years intervention activities

Communication and language
Expression

		Card 9
The activities below are graded according to difficulty. Begin with the activity described in Step 1. Move on to the next step only when the child shows confidence and success. You may find that the child progresses through the first steps quickly. It is important to provide opportunities for the child to practice the activities daily.		

Observed behaviour	• Inability to hold a simple conversation (age-related expectation at 36 months). • Inability to convey thoughts and ideas coherently. • Uses very little intonation in speech.
Focus	• To extend ideas and sentences in conversation.
Activity/ Strategy	To encourage the child to improve vocabulary, sentence structure and intonation. **Step 1** The adult chooses a picture story book. The adult sits next to the child in a quiet area and asks the child to say what they see in the picture on the first page. The adult should accept their answer and then model an extended version, e.g. Child: "*Bird in tree*." Adult: "Yes, the bird is in the tree". The adult and child continue to do this throughout the book. The adult should avoid asking questions about the picture. The adult points to a character or object. If the child needs help describing what they see, then the adult will point to a character or object and model a phrase, e.g. "*The cat is chasing the dog*". This should be repeated every day for two weeks. **Step 2: Repeat** Step 1 is to be repeated but this time, the adult encourages the child to repeat every phrase that the adult models. Encourage the child to use more words when they are talking and to copy the intonation used on single words and phrases. **Step 3: Extend** The adult observes the child in play and in conversation or periodically asks them a question. The adult will gently encourage them to "use more words".
Assessment	• Observe the child in conversation with both adults and peers.
Outcome	• The child's vocabulary and sentences will be developing and lengthening and they will be speaking with more intonation. • Use the Intervention Record Sheet to record evidence of progress.
Resources	• Picture story book. • Intervention Record Sheet.

If the child continues to have significant difficulty in achieving a particular skill and evidence indicates they are making insufficient or no progress after four weeks of intervention you should consider consulting the school or setting SENDco.

Communication and language
Listening and attention

Listening and attention difficulties are, in most cases, the result of an underlying issue: the main causes being language and communication difficulties, hearing loss or, in some cases, difficulties with coordination and movement.

All of these factors can cause significant difficulties with attention, concentration and listening. Children may present as fidgety when sitting, fast and flighty around the classroom or simply passive, gazing into space and generally unable to sustain attention for more than a few seconds. It is important to establish the underlying cause before the appropriate intervention can be applied. The following intervention is based around communication and language difficulty.

Card 10

Observed behaviour	• May not appear to hear. • Doesn't respond to greetings. • Fleeting eye contact.
Focus	• To support the child to make eye contact and listen.
Activity/ Strategy	To encourage the child to **stop**, **look** and **listen**. Before working with the child, the adult makes a card showing a stop sign. **Step 1** When the child arrives in the setting, the adult meets them at the door of the classroom, says the child's name and shows the child the **stop** sign. The **stop** sign is very important. The adult then offers a greeting. This can be a "*hello*" or a wave. The child is encouraged to respond to the greeting before moving off. **Step 2** Repeat Step 1 as the child moves around the classroom. The adult then gives them a simple task to complete. **Step 3** In the outdoor area (where there are lots of distractions), the adult repeats Steps 1 and 2. The adult must wait until the child stops and shows that they are ready to listen by making eye contact. Before speaking to the child it is important to note that for some children eye contact may be difficult. They may focus on something else while listening.
Assessment	• Observe the child responding to Step 1. Offer praise and reward for success. • Use the Intervention Record Sheet to record evidence of progress.
Outcome	• The child will stop and look at an adult when being spoken to.
Resources	• Stop sign. • PSA Card 5. • Intervention Record Sheet.

If the child continues to have significant difficulty in achieving a particular skill and evidence indicates they are making insufficient or no progress after four weeks of intervention you should consider consulting the school or setting SENDco.

Communication and language
Listening and attention

		Card 11
The activities below are graded according to difficulty. Begin with the activity described in Step 1. Move on to the next step only when the child shows confidence and success. You may find that the child progresses through the first steps quickly. It is important to provide opportunities for the child to practice the activities daily.		

Observed behaviour	• Presents attention and listening difficulties. • Compared to their peers, they are unable to maintain attention. • Only able to concentrate for very short periods of time.
Focus	• To extend the child's attention and listening skills.
Activity/ Strategy	To sit, look and listen during carpet time for a longer period of time. Before working with the child, the adult makes symbol cards to represent "good looking" (eyes card), "good listening" (ear card) and "good sitting" (child sitting on the floor). **Step 1** The adult must check that the child has a comfortable sitting position on the carpet. Some children may need additional support, e.g. resting their back against a wall with their legs stretched out or provide a chair for them to sit on. Introduce to the class the symbols "good listening", "good looking" and "good sitting". The adult models "good listening", "good looking" and "good sitting". **Step 2** Introduce a one-minute sand timer and ask the child to sit on the carpet, look at the adult and listen to what they are saying, until the sand runs through the timer. The child may look at the timer initially and not at the adult—this is to be expected. **Step 3** The adult displays the symbol cards on the wall where they can be clearly seen by the child. At the beginning of each carpet time the adult points to the symbol cards and reminds the child about "good looking", "good sitting" and "good listening". The adult turns over the three-minute sand timer and encourages the child to "sit", "look" and listen at least until the sand runs out. The adult encourages the child not to watch the sand timer. **Step 4: The challenge** Repeat Step 3 using a five-minute timer and extend further as appropriate.
Assessment	• Observe the child sitting on the carpet prior to Step 1. • Use the Intervention Record Sheet to record evidence of progress.
Outcome	• The child will have improved their sitting, looking and listening skills.
Resources	• Sitting, looking and listening symbol cards. • Sand timers. • PSA Card 3. • Intervention Record Sheet.

If the child continues to have significant difficulty in achieving a particular skill and evidence indicates they are making insufficient or no progress after four weeks of intervention you should consider consulting the school or setting SENDco.

The early years intervention activities | **29**

Communication and language
Listening and attention

		Card 12
The activities below are graded according to difficulty. Begin with the activity described in Step 1. Move on to the next step only when the child shows confidence and success. You may find that the child progresses through the first steps quickly. It is important to provide opportunities for the child to practice the activities daily.		

Observed behaviour	• Shifts attention from one thing to another.
Focus	• To improve concentration.
Activity/ Strategy	To spend more time at an activity before moving on. **Step 1** Before working with the child, the adult makes a personal planning board and a posting box (see description below in the Resource section). The adult shows the child five photographs or pictures that represent an activity within the classroom, for example, a car. The adult asks the child to choose three favourite activities represented by the photographs/pictures. They then put the photographs/pictures in the boxes of the personal planning board. The adult will ask the child to look at the planning board and choose where they want to play. The child then begins the activity. The adult will display a one-minute sand timer. When the sand has run out, the child should be encouraged to stop the activity and get ready to move on. Then the child can take the card that represents the activity they have completed from the planner and post it in the posting box. They are then asked to choose another activity, stay and play for one minute. Repeat for the final activity on the planner. **Step 2** Repeat Step 1 but extend the time the child stays and plays for three minutes. **Step 3** Provide the child with a planning board and a wider range of photographs/picture cards. Encourage the child to use the planner independently. **Step 4: The challenge** The adult provides a five-minute timer and supports the child to stay and play at each activity for five minutes.
Assessment	• Observe the child using their planner independently. • Use the Intervention Record Sheet to record evidence of progress.
Outcome	• The child will be able to choose an activity, stay and play for five minutes.
Resources	• Personal planning board with three squares, each having a strip of Velcro in the middle. • A set of photograph/picture cards of classroom activities with Velcro on the back. • A "posting box", e.g. a shoe box covered in paper with a slit cut into the lid. • Sand timers—1, 3 and 5 minutes. • Intervention Record Sheet.

If the child continues to have significant difficulty in achieving a particular skill and evidence indicates they are making insufficient or no progress after four weeks of intervention you should consider consulting the school or setting SENDco.

Communication and language
Listening and attention

The steps below are graded according to success. Begin with the activity described in Step 1. Move on to the next step only if the strategy appears not to be as effective as you had hoped. You may find that the child improves because of the strategy in the first step—there may be no need to move on to the remaining steps. It is important to provide appropriate resources for the child every time he is expected to sit still.		**Card 13**

Observed behaviour	• Inability to sit still, fidgets, easily distracted.
Focus	• To improve the child's ability to sit still.
Activity/ Strategy	To sit on the carpet with reasonable control of movement. **Step 1** When the child is sitting on the carpet, make sure they are in a supportive, comfortable sitting position, e.g. resting their back against a wall with their legs stretched out if they need to or sitting on a chair. The adult provides an object for the child to "fiddle" with. If this improves the child's ability to sit with control of movement, then continue this intervention. The child may always need to sit in this position. Move to the next step only if necessary. **Step 2** Give the child a heavy object to place on their knees, for example a novelty weighted doorstop, weighted cushion or a drawstring bag filled with beanbags. This will put weight on their legs and make it easier for them to keep still whilst they are listening. **Step 3** The adult will provide the child with a range of intervention aids such as a weighted doorstop, weighted cushion, fiddle toys or a beanbag sack. The child will select their space for sitting and choose the intervention aid that they want to use. The adult gradually increases the time the child sits.
Assessment	• Observe the child after Steps 1, 2 and 3. • Use the Intervention Record Sheet to record evidence of progress.
Outcome	• The child will sit still with more control of movement.
Resources	• A heavy object such as a book or catalogue, a novelty doorstop, weighted blanket, weighted cushion, a drawstring bag filled with beanbags. • Sand timers. • PSA Card 4. • Intervention Record Sheet.
If the child continues to have significant difficulty in achieving a particular skill and evidence indicates they are making insufficient or no progress after four weeks of intervention you should consider consulting the school or setting SENDco.	

The early years intervention activities | **31**

Communication and language
Listening and attention

		Card 14
The activities below are graded according to difficulty. Begin with the activity described in Step 1. Move on to the next step only when the child shows confidence and success. You may find that the child progresses through the first steps quickly. It is important to provide opportunities for the child to practice the activities daily.		

Observed behaviour	• May talk continuously and doesn't appear to understand the rules of conversation.
Focus	• To improve conversational skills, encouraging waiting and turn-taking.
Activity/ Strategy	Model the rules of conversation. Before working with the child, the adult makes symbol cards to represent **waiting** (clock card), **listening** (ear card) and **continue** (thumbs up). **Step 1** The adult shows the child the three symbols: *clock, ear* and *thumbs up*. The adult demonstrates what the symbols represent by saying a nursery rhyme. Halfway through the nursery rhyme they will then hold the *clock card* up and immediately stop talking and listen. The adult then holds up the *thumbs up* card and continues the nursery rhyme. The adult will ask the child to say a nursery rhyme and the adult will use the symbol cards to encourage the child to wait and listen. The adult will then hold up the thumbs up card and the child continues the nursery rhyme. The adult should do this with the child two or three times every day. **Step 2** The adult shows the child a picture. Ask them to think of three important things to say about the picture, but **only** three. After the child has said three things about the picture, the adult then holds up the *clock* symbol. They then hold up the *ear* symbol and at the same time they turn over the 30-second sand timer. During this time, the adult comments on the picture. After 30 seconds, the adult stops talking and the *thumbs up* card is shown. **Step 3** The adult engages the child in conversation. Choose a topic of particular interest to them. The adult asks them to think of three important things they want to tell you. Use the *clock, ear, thumbs up* symbols and the timer regularly to reinforce the meaning of waiting, listening and turn-taking during a conversation. Repeat this step regularly.
Assessment	• Observe the child turn-taking in conversation with the help of the prompt symbols. • Use the Intervention Record Sheet to record evidence of progress.
Outcome	• The child has improved their conversational skills.
Resources	• Set of symbol cards: *clock, ear* and *thumbs up.* • 30 second sand timer. • Intervention Record Sheet.

If the child continues to have significant difficulty in achieving a particular skill and evidence indicates they are making insufficient or no progress after four weeks of intervention you should consider consulting the school or setting SENDco.

The early years intervention activities

Communication and language
Listening and attention

		Card 15
The activities below are graded according to difficulty. Begin with the activity described in Step 1. Move on to the next step only when the child shows confidence and success. You may find that the child progresses through the first steps quickly. It is important to provide opportunities for the child to practice the activities daily.		

Observed behaviour	• May be quiet and withdrawn. • May play in isolation.
Focus	• To encourage social interaction.
Activity/ Strategy	To play a turn-taking part in an activity with another child without adult support. **Step 1** The adult will show the child photographs of the children in the class (perhaps at the planning board if photographs are displayed). The child is prompted to choose a child they would like to play with. The adult selects an appropriate turn-taking game and the adult and the two children sit in a quiet area of the room. The adult begins the game and models the language required for turn-taking, e.g. "*Whose turn is it next*" or "*It's . . . turn next*". The adult and children play the game. **Step 2** The adult prepares the game for the two children but this time does not play with them. The adult reminds the children of the rules of the game and only intervenes when necessary to encourage communication between the two children. **Step 3** The adult encourages the child to go and ask another child to play a turn-taking game with them. The adult encourages independent turn-taking. **Step 4: The challenge** The adult shows the child a selection of turn-taking games. The child is encouraged to choose one game. The child is then asked to choose a child to play the game with.
Assessment	• Observe the child independently playing a turn-taking game with another child. • Use the Intervention Record Sheet to record evidence of progress.
Outcome	• The child will seek other children to play with.
Resources	• A selection of turn-taking games/activities. • Intervention Record Sheet.
If the child continues to have significant difficulty in achieving a particular skill and evidence indicates they are making insufficient or no progress after four weeks of intervention you should consider consulting the school or setting SENDco.	

The early years intervention activities   **33**

Supporting receptive language and communication through the environment

	Research shows that at least half of all children entering primary school have speech, language and communication needs. Therefore it is important to support and develop children's communication in their learning environments. The following inclusive strategies, if applied consistently and systematically, will support children to become successful and effective verbal or non-verbal communicators.	**Card 16**

Observed behaviour	• Child presenting with a range of communication difficulties as identified in the Checklist of Observed Behaviours.
Focus	• To support the child's confident and independent communication by embedding supportive, inclusive teaching strategies and developing a communication-friendly environment.
Strategies	**Speaking:** • Always allow time: try not to jump in too soon or finish the child's sentence for them. • Support the child's talking with non-verbal communication where necessary, e.g. use visual signs and symbols. • Comment on what the child is doing rather than ask too many questions. Remember the ratio of four comments to one question. • Model and expand on what the child says. • Always value the child's contribution and demonstrate patience. **Understanding:** • When giving instructions, reinforce understanding and support verbal communication with photographs, gestures or visual signs or symbols. • Consider introducing simple signing, for example Makaton. • Always use simple words and phrases. Try not to overload the child with too much language. • ALWAYS prompt the child to show their understanding of communication with thumbs up or a nod of the head. • ALWAYS display a visual timetable and refer to it regularly throughout the day. This helps the child to feel and understand what is happening next in the daily routine. A string and bead stretched below the timetable helps to show time passing. • Support the child who watches and copies others by communicating individually with the child. • Provide visual, interactive activities to support understanding during carpet and group times. **Listening and attention:** • The child's age plus three is the average length of time for children to attend and listen. • Teach "good sitting" and "good listening". Use visual prompts, holding or displaying them where the child can see them clearly. Remind the child about what you expect them to do. Some children may require an alternative seating arrangement (see Intervention Activity 11, Step 1, Page 28). • Use a sand timer for a given time to show the child that time is passing and that you would like them to sit or listen until the sand runs through the timer. It may be a 30-second or 1-minute timer to begin with. • Offer the child a toy to fiddle with. • Provide the child with a weighted object to help reduce fidgeting. • For older reception children, prepare a dish and a single Lego model. For every few seconds that the child sits appropriately and listens, reward them with one or more of the Lego pieces. If they successfully collect all the Lego pieces, they can build the model after the carpet session is finished. Gradually lengthen the time between awarding the model pieces to encourage the child to sit a little longer. • NB the child may initially concentrate only on collecting the model pieces. Be consistent with the strategy and you will gradually support the child to listen appropriately.
Assessment	• Observe how the child responds to the strategies. • Use the Intervention Record Sheet to record evidence of progress.
Outcome	• The child will begin to communicate with confidence and independence.
Resources	• Visual resources. • Sand timer. • Lego models. • Weighted objects. • Fiddle toys. • Intervention Record Sheet.

34 The early years intervention activities

Supporting receptive language and communication through the environment

Card 17

Research shows that at least half of all children entering primary school have speech language and communication needs.

Therefore it is important to support and develop children's communication in their learning environments. The following inclusive strategies, if applied consistently and systematically, will support children to become successful and effective verbal or non-verbal communicators.

Observed behaviour	• Children presenting with a range of communication difficulties as identified in the Initial Frame of Reference.
Focus	• To support the child's confident and independent communication by embedding supportive, inclusive teaching strategies and developing a communication-friendly environment.
Strategies	**Labelling** • Use large, simple, clear symbols to label all the learning areas. • Display them on a muted background with space around the label. • Clearly label all resource trays, boxes, cupboards, drawers etc. with clear photographs of the resource and the name of the resource. • Avoid photographs that carry a lot of unnecessary information, for example Lego on a table with children standing around the table. **Displays** • Use muted colours for display backgrounds. • Keep displays simple and clear. Ensure that they only contain the information that you want children to know about. **LESS IS MORE.** **Visual resources** • Always display your visual timetable where it can be clearly seen by all children. If the room is L-shaped or has hidden corners, then consider displaying a timetable in more than one area. • Display and carry clear visual black and white symbols representing the behaviour you expect from the children, e.g. *walking*, *sharing*, *being kind and friendly*, *sitting*, etc. Show them frequently to children to remind or reward them. • Use sand timers to help children wait their turn, sit on the carpet etc. **Gaining children's attention** Before communicating with children, always gain their attention first. Consider: • Shaking a tambourine or a shaker—something with a *distinctive* rather than loud sound. • Turning the lights on and off (to support the child with low levels of hearing). • Wiggling fingers helps to gain attention. • Wait for all children to "look" before communicating. • Verbally give a clear, simple instruction, but always accompany it with a visual symbol and/or gesture. • Gain acknowledgement of understanding by "thumbs up".
Assessment	• Observe how children respond to the strategies. • Use the Intervention Record Sheet to record evidence of progress.
Outcome	• Children will begin to respond to communication with increasing confidence and independence.
Resources	• Visual resources. • Sand timer. • Tambourine. • Shaker. • Intervention Record Sheet.

Physical development
Moving and handling

		Card 18
The activities below are graded according to difficulty. Begin with the activity described in Step 1. Move on to the next step only when the child shows confidence and success. You may find that the child progresses through the first steps quickly. It is important to provide opportunities for the child to practice the activities daily. This will maximise their development and secure the memory of specific movements.		

Observed behaviour	• Walks awkwardly or frequently trips. • Prefers to run rather than walk.
Focus	• To improve balance and stability. • To slow gross movements.
Activity/Strategy	To walk along a straight line with controlled movements. **Step 1** The adult designs a straight pathway using two strips of masking tape about 20cm apart within the indoor or outdoor environment. The adult asks the child to walk between the lines. The child is encouraged to stay on the pathway, walking between the two strips of tape. Initially the child may need some help. Remember to make it a game, use the child's interests. **Step 2** The adult supports the child to walk backwards along the pathway between the lines. **Step 3** The adult reduces the width of the pathway. **Step 4: The challenge** Design a curved pathway as a "route" for the child to follow either within the indoor or outdoor environment.
Assessment	• Observe the child completing the activities. Offer praise and reward for success. Set achievable challenges, e.g. *"How far can you get without wobbling off the line?"*. • Use the Intervention Record Sheet to record evidence of progress.
Outcome	• The child walks with more control around the environment.
Resources	• Masking tape, string, rope or similar. • PSA Card 6. • Intervention Record Sheet.
If the child continues to have significant difficulty in achieving a particular skill and evidence indicates they are making insufficient or no progress after four weeks of intervention you should consider consulting the school or setting SENDco.	

Physical development
Moving and handling

		Card 19
The activities below are graded according to difficulty. Begin with the activity described in Step 1. Move on to the next step only when the child shows confidence and success. You may find that the child progresses through the first steps quickly. It is important to provide opportunities for the child to practice the activities daily. This will maximise their development and secure the memory of specific movements.		

Observed behaviour	• Walks awkwardly or frequently trips. • Prefers to run rather than walk.
Focus	• To improve balance and stability. • To slow gross movements.
Activity/Strategy	To walk along a slightly raised wide bench or balance beam. **Step 1** The adult asks the child to walk along a bench or balance beam. The adult must avoid holding the child's hand as this will affect the child's sense of balance. If the child does require support then either lightly hold the child's waist from behind and encourage the child to put their arms out to the side. Gradually reduce the support by either holding onto the child's t-shirt with two hands or use a scarf around their waist, holding the two ends of the scarf at the centre of their back. Repeat this daily until the adult feels the child is confident enough to move to Step 2. **Step 2** Raise the bench if possible and repeat Step 1. The adult will encourage the child to walk along independently. Only give support where absolutely necessary. **Step 3** Raise one end of the bench or beam and encourage the child to walk up and walk down it. **Step 4: The challenge** How far or quickly can the child walk without wobbling off the bench or beam? Can they walk backwards?
Assessment	• Observe the child completing the activities. Offer praise and reward for success. • Use the Intervention Record Sheet to record evidence of progress.
Outcome	• The child balances with increased independence and confidence.
Resources	• Wide bench or beam. • PSA Card 6. • Intervention Record Sheet.

If the child continues to have significant difficulty in achieving a particular skill and evidence indicates they are making insufficient or no progress after four weeks of intervention you should consider consulting the school or setting SENDco.

Physical development
Moving and handling

The activities below are graded according to difficulty. Begin with the activity described in Step 1. Move on to the next step only when the child shows confidence and success. You may find that the child progresses through the first steps quickly. It is important to provide opportunities for the child to practice the activities daily. This will maximise their development and secure the memory of specific movements.		**Card 20**

Observed behaviour	• Walks awkwardly or frequently trips. • Prefers to run rather than walk.
Focus	• To improve balance and stability. • To slow gross movements.
Activity/Strategy	To step one foot at a time with controlled movements. **Step 1** The adult arranges six flat dinner-plate-sized "stepping stones" in a straight line or a circle on the floor. The child is encouraged to step onto each "stone", ensuring both feet are firmly on the stone before moving to the next "stone". The child should be able to do this independently. Remember – avoid holding the child's hand as a means of support. If the child does require support then either lightly hold the child's waist from behind and encourage the child to put their arms out to the side. Gradually reduce the support by either holding onto the child's t-shirt with two hands or use a scarf around his waist, holding the two ends of the scarf at the centre of their back. **Step 2** Support the child to walk across the "stepping stones" and encourage the child to step with one foot only on each stone. **Step 3** Provide footprints and repeat Step 2, encouraging the child to put one foot onto one footprint. **Step 4: The challenge** Can the child walk across raised stepping stones (washing up bowls on a non-slip surface) without wobbling?
Assessment	• Observe the child completing the activities. Offer praise and reward for success. • Use the Intervention Record Sheet to record evidence of progress.
Outcome	• The child has improved balance and confidence.
Resources	• Stepping stones—carpet squares, felt circles work best on most surfaces. Ensure non-slip surfaces. • Footprints—paper or card footprints the size of an adult's foot. • Raised stepping stones—washing up bowls. • PSA Card 6. • Intervention Record Sheet.

If the child continues to have significant difficulty in achieving a particular skill and evidence indicates they are making insufficient or no progress after four weeks of intervention you should consider consulting the school or setting SENDco.

The early years intervention activities

Physical development
Moving and handling

The activities below are graded according to difficulty. Begin with the activity described in Step 1. Move on to the next step only when the child shows confidence and success. You may find that the child progresses through the first steps quickly. It is important to provide opportunities for the child to practice the activities daily. This will maximise their development and secure the memory of specific movements.	**Card 21**

Observed behaviour	• Has difficulty negotiating space or demonstrates poor spatial awareness. • Often bumps into things.
Focus	• Spatial awareness.
Activity/ Strategy	To be aware of where their body parts are and where they are in relation to objects and other people. **Step 1** The adult and child play body part games and songs. To include head, arms, feet, legs and body, e.g. The Hokey Cokey (stamp your foot, nod your head, wave your arm, and shake your leg). **Step 2** The adult lays two ropes on the floor. The adult asks the child to walk between the ropes then either side of the rope. Encourage the child NOT to touch the rope with their feet. **Step 3** Place a hula-hoop on the floor. The adult asks the child to step in and out of the hoop, first slowly, then a little quicker. Ask the child to then circle around the outside of the hoop stepping in and out. Add some clapping as the child gets more confident, e.g. as the child steps in, clap once and as the child steps out, clap again. **Step 4: The challenge** Place five cones in a row and place a beanbag on the top of each cone. Ask the child to weave in and out of the cones and collect the beanbags, then turn around, weave through the cones again and place the beanbags back on top of each cone.
Assessment	• Observe the child completing the activities. Offer praise and reward for success. • Use the Intervention Record Sheet to record evidence of progress.
Outcome	• The child is able to negotiate space more successfully and reduces the number of trips and bumps.
Resources	• Ropes. • Hula-hoops. • Cones. • Beanbags. • PSA Card 6. • Intervention Record Sheet.

If the child continues to have significant difficulty in achieving a particular skill and evidence indicates they are making insufficient or no progress after four weeks of intervention you should consider consulting the school or setting SENDco.

Physical development
Moving and handling

The activities below are graded according to difficulty. Begin with the activity described in Step 1. Move on to the next step only when the child shows confidence and success. You may find that the child progresses through the first steps quickly. It is important to provide opportunities for the child to practice the activities daily. This will maximise their development and secure the memory of specific movements.		**Card 22**

Observed behaviour	• Difficulty with pedaling a tricycle or similar toy.
Focus	• Bilateral integration.
Activity/ Strategy	To enable the limbs on the right side of the body to work in combination or in opposition to the left limbs. **Step 1** Encourage the child to creep and crawl. The adult provides play tunnels, large cardboard boxes, blankets, chairs, tables. The adult asks the child to crawl forwards, backwards, in and out of . . . ? Can the child commando creep? **Step 2** Play **Blowfish**. The adult makes a paper fish and places it on a large smooth surface. The child is asked to get onto their hands and knees, blow the fish and crawl after it. This is a great inclusive group activity. **Step 3** The adult asks the child to stand behind a chair. Turn sideways and hold onto the chair with one hand. Ask the child to bring one knee up and then lower it, but not place the foot on the floor. Repeat several times then ask the child to turn around, put the other hand on the chair and raise the other leg. Ask the child not to touch the floor with the foot they are lifting. **Step 4: The challenge** Place six hoops in a straight line. Ask the child to step into the first hoop with their right foot and hop, then step into the next hoop with their left foot and hop. Ask the child to repeat this and step, hop into the other hoops. The action is right step hop, left step hop!
Assessment	• Observe the child completing the activities. Offer praise and reward for success. • Use the Intervention Record Sheet to record evidence of progress.
Outcome	• To show increased limb coordination.
Resources	• Tunnels. • Cardboard boxes. • Blankets. • Paper fish—about 20 cm long. • Chair. • Hoops. • PSA Card 9. • Intervention Record Sheet.

If the child continues to have significant difficulty in achieving a particular skill and evidence indicates they are making insufficient or no progress after four weeks of intervention you should consider consulting the school or setting SENDco.

The early years intervention activities

Physical development
Moving and handling

		Card 23
The activities below are graded according to difficulty. Begin with the activity described in Exercise 1. Move on to the next step only when the child shows confidence and success. You may find that the child progresses through the first steps quickly. It is important to provide opportunities for the child to practice the activities daily. This will maximise their development and secure the memory of specific movements.		

Observed behaviour	• Prefers to lie rather than sit on carpet. • Unable to sustain an upright sitting position. • Has difficulty in getting from a sitting position to a standing position.
Focus	• Core strengthening.
Activity/ Strategy	Three exercises to strengthen the core muscles needed for good sitting and good posture. **Exercise 1** **Tiddly wink teaser** The child lies on their back on a PE mat with their knees bent. The adult places a tiddly wink or counter on the child's left knee. The child reaches up to collect the counter with their left hand and places it in a bowl which is next to their left hand. The adult then places another counter on the right knee for the child to reach with their right hand and moves the bowl to the right side. This is repeated ten times. The adult can then ask the child to reach across their body to collect a counter from their right knee with their left hand and repeat with their right hand reaching across to their left knee. **Exercise 2** **Bean bag balance** Ask the child to collect a bean bag from a basket and put the bean bag on their head. Encourage the child to walk with the bean bag on their head towards an empty basket. The child places the bean bag into the empty basket. Repeat this several times. Gradually increase the distance between the two baskets. **Exercise 3** **Wibbly wobbly** Help the child to sit on top of a large gym ball. Encourage the child to grip the ball with their knees and try to stay on the ball without falling off. **The challenge** **Superman** Ask the child to lie across the gym ball on their tummy and stretch their arms out in front of them like Superman. How long can they hold that position?
Assessment	• Observe the child completing the activities. Offer praise and reward for success. • Note the level of support the child requires to begin with during each of the exercises and comment on the development of their stability and confidence. • Use the Intervention Record Sheet to record evidence of progress.
Outcome	• The child is able to support themself in a sitting position for longer periods.
Resources	• PE mat. • Counters. • Bowls. • Bean bags. • Baskets or tubs. • Gym ball. • Intervention Record Sheet.

If the child continues to have significant difficulty in achieving a particular skill and evidence indicates they are making insufficient or no progress after four weeks of intervention you should consider consulting the school or setting SENDco.

Physical development
Moving and handling

The activities below are graded according to difficulty. Begin with the activity described in Step 1. Move on to the next step only when the child shows confidence and success. You may find that the child progresses through the first steps quickly. It is important to provide opportunities for the child to practice the activities daily.		**Card 24**

Observed behaviour	• Unable to hold a pencil between thumb and finger and make controlled marks (age-related expectations at 50 months).
Focus	• To develop a tripod pencil grip.
Activity/Strategy	To strengthen finger and wrist muscles. **Step 1** Encourage the child to access a "finger fun" area (see resource list below) for at least ten minutes per day. The adult models how to use the resources. This will help to strengthen the muscles in the child's hands and wrists. **Step 2** The adult sits next to the child and provides large plastic tweezers, ten cotton balls and a container. The adult shows the child how to hold the tweezers correctly (between thumb and forefinger) and demonstrates how to pick up a cotton ball with the tweezers and transfer it to the container. The adult then asks the child to copy the action, transferring all ten cotton balls into the container. **Step 3** The adult provides the child with a smaller pair of tweezers, some raisins and a container. Step 1 is repeated using the smaller tweezers and raisins. **Step 4** The adult provides some raisins and a bowl. The child is then asked to pick the raisins up one by one between finger and thumb and put them into the bowl. **Step 5: The challenge** The adult asks the child to pick up a range of small objects between finger and thumb, e.g. small beads, dried peas, etc.
Assessment	• Observe the child's pincer movements. • Use the Intervention Record Sheet to record evidence of progress.
Outcome	• The child will have strengthened the muscles in the fingers and memorised the pincer movement.
Resources	• Ten cotton balls, large plastic tweezers, small plastic tweezers, raisins, dried peas, etc. and a container. • Finger fun table—bubble wrap, play dough, jars with screw tops, pegs and washing line, nuts and bolts, etc. • PSA Card 7. • Intervention Record Sheet.

If the child continues to have significant difficulty in achieving a particular skill and evidence indicates they are making insufficient or no progress after four weeks of intervention you should consider consulting the school or setting SENDco.

The early years intervention activities

Physical development
Moving and handling

Card 25

	The activities below are graded according to difficulty. Begin with the activity described in Step 1. Move on to the next step only when the child shows confidence and success. You may find that the child progresses through the first steps quickly. It is important to provide opportunities for the child to practice the activities daily.
Observed behaviour	• Shows difficulty in cutting. • Shows difficulty in threading (age-related expectation at 50 months).
Focus	• To develop fine motor coordination.
Activity/ Strategy	To strengthen muscles in fingers and wrists. **Step 1** Provide a selection of "finger fun" resources and display them on a table in the classroom (see resource list below). The adult will encourage and accompany the child, spending ten minutes twice a day at this table. The adult will model how to use the resources and ask the child to copy, e.g. popping bubble wrap between each finger and thumb, picking cotton buds with tweezers, etc. **Step 2** • Provide the child with a long straw or a thin strip of A4 paper and a pair of "sprung" handled scissors. Ask the child to "snip" the straw or strip of paper into small pieces. • Ask the child to roll play dough into a thin sausage shape. They then snip the dough into small pieces. Provide a range of scissors for the child to snip with before moving on to cutting. • Provide the child with large threading equipment (see resource list below). Demonstrate to the child how to thread. Ask the child to thread some cut-up cardboard tubing onto a piece of dowelling. **Step 3** • The adult draws straight or curved thick lines onto a piece of paper. Provide the child with a choice of scissors. The child then selects the scissors they prefer to use. Ask the child to cut along the lines. • Provide the child with a range of threading equipment (see resource list) and support the child to thread. **The challenge** The adult will ask the child to cut out a circle or a square using scissors of their choice and make a wiggly snake using a lace and bead. **Note: to develop fine motor coordination, always start BIG and aim towards SMALL. Success requires lots of daily practice and over-learning of the skill.**
Assessment	• Observe the child completing the activities and monitor the development of fine motor coordination over time. • Use the Intervention Record Sheet to record evidence of progress.
Outcome	• The child will be able to successfully use scissors for cutting, and thread beads onto a lace.
Resources	• Finger Fun resources—bubble wrap, tweezers (large and small), cotton wool balls, raisins, jars with lids, unifix cubes, pegs, play dough. • Cutting—"sprung" scissors, double-handled scissors, training scissors, play dough and paper to snip and cut. • Threading—strips of wooden dowelling, cut-up cardboard tubing, plastic washing line, cotton reels, long pipe cleaners, laces with long rigid ends, large holed beads. • PSA Card 8. • Intervention Record Sheet.
	If the child continues to have significant difficulty in achieving a particular skill and evidence indicates they are making insufficient or no progress after four weeks of intervention you should consider consulting the school or setting SENDco.

The early years intervention activities | **43**

Physical development
Moving and handling

		Card 26
The activities below are graded according to difficulty. Begin with the activity described in Step 1. Move on to the next step only when the child shows confidence and success. You may find that the child progresses through the first steps quickly. It is important to provide opportunities for the child to practice the activities daily.		

Observed behaviour	• Avoidance of small construction toys such as jigsaws or building blocks.
Focus	• To develop fine motor coordination and confidence.
Activity/ Strategy	To build confidence and success in using small construction toys or jigsaws. **Step 1a** The adult sits beside the child with a six-piece inset puzzle with four pieces already in place. The adult asks the child to complete the puzzle. The child is encouraged to put the last two pieces in the puzzle. The adult and child celebrate the completion of the puzzle. Repeat with a range of six-piece puzzles. **Step 1b** The adult sits beside the child with five magnetic bricks. Stack three bricks into a tower. The adult asks the child to add two more bricks to the tower. The adult and child celebrate the building of the tower. **Step 2** Repeat Steps 1a and 1b. The adult reduces the number of puzzle pieces and bricks already in place. The child is asked to gradually place more jigsaw pieces in the puzzle or add more bricks to build a higher tower. Continue this step until the child is able to complete a six-piece jigsaw independently and build a tower of five bricks independently. **Step 3: The challenge** The child is supported to complete an eight- or ten-piece inset puzzle and is asked to build a tower of eight magnetic bricks. Non-magnetic bricks may be introduced at this stage, however the child may need to begin at Step1b.
Assessment	• Observe how confidently the child attempts the activity. • Use the Intervention Record Sheet to record evidence of progress.
Outcome	• The child will confidently complete a small inset puzzle and construct a small tower of bricks.
Resources	• A range of wooden inset puzzles. • Magnetic bricks. • Wooden bricks. • Intervention Record Sheet.

If the child continues to have significant difficulty in achieving a particular skill and evidence indicates they are making insufficient or no progress after four weeks of intervention you should consider consulting the school or setting SENDco.

Physical development
Health and self care

The activities below are graded according to difficulty. Begin with the activity described in Step 1. Move on to the next step only when the child shows confidence and success. You may find that the child progresses through the first steps quickly. It is important to provide opportunities for the child to practice the activities daily.		**Card 27**

Observed behaviour	• May prefer to eat with fingers. • Continued messy eating, struggles to eat with cutlery.
Focus	• To develop the ability to use a knife, fork and spoon.
Activity/ Strategy	To cut, stab and scoop with cutlery. **Step 1: Using a spoon** The adult sits with the child at a table. The adult makes sure the child is sitting on a chair of the correct size, feet firmly on the floor at a table that is the correct height. The adult provides two bowls: one filled with sand and one empty. Ask the child to "scoop" the sand with the spoon and pour it into the empty bowl. The adult may have to demonstrate. **Step 2: Using a fork** The adult provides 20 small balls of play dough, a fork and two plates. The play dough balls are placed on one plate. The adult demonstrates stabbing the dough with a fork, picking it up and putting it on the empty plate. You may have to use fingers to remove the dough from the fork. The adult then asks the child to do the same. **Step 3: Using a knife** The adult provides a long sausage-shaped length of play dough, a knife and a wooden cutting board. The adult demonstrates cutting the playdough into small pieces. Stab the dough with a fork to hold it in place then cut with the knife. Ask the child to do the same. **Step 4: Altogether** The adult asks the child to practice the skills learned with real food. Use chopped-up set jelly to scoop with a spoon and a banana to cut with a knife and fork. **Step 5: The challenge—fork/spoon to mouth** Provide the child with jelly and a banana or similar food that is easy to scoop and cut. Put the food on a plate and provide a knife, fork and spoon. Encourage the child to eat the banana with a knife and fork followed by eating the jelly with a spoon. The steps should be carried out every day until the skill is mastered.
Assessment	• Observe the child scooping, stabbing and cutting food with cutlery. • Use the Intervention Record Sheet to record evidence of progress.
Outcome	• The child will be able to eat food with a knife, fork and spoon.
Resources	• Two plates. • Wooden chopping board. • Rigid knife, fork and spoon. • Two bowls. • Play dough. • Sand. • Jelly. • Banana or other similar food. • Intervention Record Sheet.

If the child continues to have significant difficulty in achieving a particular skill and evidence indicates they are making insufficient or no progress after four weeks of intervention you should consider consulting the school or setting SENDco.

Physical development
Health and self care

The activities below are graded according to difficulty. Begin with the activity described in Step 1. Move on to the next step only when the child shows confidence and success. You may find that the child progresses through the first steps quickly. It is important to provide opportunities for the child to practice the activities daily.		**Card 28**

Observed behaviour	• Struggles with dressing.
Focus	• For the child to independently put their coat or shirt on.
Activity/ Strategy	To increase independence in getting dressed. **Step 1: Coat sleeves** The adult gives the child six rubber or plastic quoits. The adult also has six quoits and shows the child how to put the rings/quoits one by one onto one arm. The child is then asked to copy this action, threading their arm through each quoit and pulling it to the top of the arm. This can be used as a counting game or a colour recognition game. The adult then demonstrates how to remove the quoits. This time the quoits are removed all at once (allow the quoits to fall to the floor). This action is repeated with the other arm. This activity will give the child experience of pulling something up their arm resembling a sleeve. **Step 2** The adult uses an adult-sized coat or shirt and demonstrates how to take hold of the collar of the coat, to hold it in place and then how to push their arm through the sleeve whilst pulling the sleeve to the top of the arm. The child is then asked to copy this action with the adult-sized coat or shirt. Repeat this action with both arms separately. This activity should be repeated daily. **Step 3** The adult will ask the child to put on the adult coat or shirt. The only support the adult will give to the child is to hold the shoulder or lapel. This will enable the child to thread the other arm into the other sleeve. The adult will then ask the child to remove the coat. **Step 4** Repeat Steps 1–3 with the child's own coat or shirt. **Step 5** Supporting the child to dress with other items of clothing. • Always begin with larger-sized clothes. • Use a hula-hoop to simulate putting on a jumper. • Ask the child to put a small hoop over their head, thread one arm up through the hoop followed by the other arm. Then take hold of the hoop with both hands and pull it down towards the floor. • Quoits can be used to stimulate putting legs into trousers.
Assessment	• Observe the child through Steps 1, 2, 3 and 4. • Use the Intervention Record Sheet to record evidence of progress.
Outcome	• The child will be able to put on their clothes independently.
Resources	• Twelve coloured quoits. • Adult-sized coat or shirt. • Child's own coat or shirt. • Hula-hoop. • PSA Card 12. • Intervention Record Sheet.

If the child continues to have significant difficulty in achieving a particular skill and evidence indicates they are making insufficient or no progress after four weeks of intervention you should consider consulting the school or setting SENDco.

The early years intervention activities

Physical development
Health and self care

		Card 29
It is important to provide opportunities for the child to practice the strategies daily. Note: If the child is still using a dummy it is imperative to work with the parent/carer to reduce and eventually completely remove the use of a dummy.		

Observed behaviour	• Excessive salivation.
Focus	• To strengthen facial and tongue muscles.
Activity/ Strategy	To exercise and tighten muscles in the mouth in order to reduce salivation. The adult provides daily opportunities for muscle exercise: • **Blowfish.** Cut out paper fish to blow along the floor. Use a large space such as the school hall. The child has to crawl along and blow the fish from one end to the other. • **Blow football.** Provide a TUF spot (builders tray). Place a goal at the opposite sides of the tray. Ask the child and a partner to blow a ping pong ball from one side to the other and try to score a goal. Mark the tray, colour the balls, etc., to make it look like a game of football. • **Blow painting.** • **Blowing bubbles.** • **Suck it up.** Ask the child to transfer paper shapes from one tray to another using a straw to suck and hold the paper. • **Lick and stick.** Make a collage with gummed paper. Lots of licking!!! • **Honey lips.** Spread honey on the child's lips then ask the child to lick them clean. • **Cheeky cheeks**. Ask the child to blow his cheeks out. Show them how to move the air from cheek to cheek. • **Funny face.** Ask the child to pull a funny face whilst looking in a mirror and hold it for five seconds building up to ten seconds. **The challenge** • How long can the child suck a ping pong ball through a straw and hold it? • How long can they hold a funny face?
Assessment	• Observe the child completing the activities. Offer praise and reward for success. • Use the Intervention Record Sheet to record evidence of progress.
Outcome	• Salivation will be reduced.
Resources	• Paper fish. • TUF spot. • Straws. • Ping pong balls. • Goals. • Gummed paper. • Honey. • Mirror. • PSA card 10. • Intervention Record Sheet.

If the child continues to have significant difficulty in achieving a particular skill and evidence indicates they are making insufficient or no progress after four weeks of intervention you should consider consulting the school or setting SENDco.

Personal, social and emotional development
Making relationships

The activities below are graded according to difficulty. Begin with the activity described in Step 1. Move on to the next step only when the child shows confidence and success. You may find that the child progresses through the first steps quickly. It is important to provide opportunities for the child to practice the activities daily.		**Card 30**

Observed behaviour	• Prefers to play in isolation. • Shows no desire to play alongside others.
Focus	• To engage in parallel play.
Activity/ Strategy	To show an interest in the activities of others. **Step 1** The adult goes to the area of the classroom that the child is in. The adult sits near (2–4ft.) to the child and models playing. **Step 2** The adult goes to the area of the classroom that the child is in. The adult sits near (2–4ft.) to the child and models playing. The adult comments on their own play, e.g. "*I am making a tower. I need a red brick*". When the child looks across or makes eye contact, the adult smiles and then comments on the child's play. **Step 3** The adult goes to the area of the classroom that the child is in. The adult sits near (2–4ft.) to the child. They have two baskets of identical resources. One basket is given to the child and the adult plays with the other basket of resources. During the play, the adult completes a running commentary on their own and the child's play. For example, "*What have we got in the basket? Oh, it's full of cars. I like the red ones. I can see you like the blue ones. . .*". **Step 4** Have two baskets of identical resources. Give the same resources to the child and to another child who is in the same area of the classroom. Complete a running commentary on the child's play.
Assessment	• Observe the child completing the activities. Offer praise and reward for success. • Use the Intervention Record Sheet to record evidence of progress.
Outcome	• The child plays side by side, watches and listens to others.
Resources	• Two baskets containing the same resources. • Intervention Record Sheet.

If the child continues to have significant difficulty in achieving a particular skill and evidence indicates they are making insufficient or no progress after four weeks of intervention you should consider consulting the school or setting SENDco.

Personal, social and emotional development
Making relationships

		Card 31
The activities below are graded according to difficulty. Begin with the activity described in Step 1. Move on to the next step only when the child shows confidence and success. You may find that the child progresses through the first steps quickly. It is important to provide opportunities for the child to practice the activities daily.		

Observed behaviour	• Shows little or no concern for other children's feelings or demonstrates an inappropriate response.
Focus	• To respond to how other children are feeling.
Activity/ Strategy	To show an appropriate response to other children. **Step 1** Show the child a selection of "feelings cards" or photographs of a familiar person showing different emotions. Show the child a card. Name and explain the emotion on the card. Can the child mimic the face? Repeat with the other cards. **Step 2** Model situations that require an appropriate response. Use four dolls or teddies to model different behaviours and responses. One teddy demonstrates the behaviour, the other three each demonstrate a different response, one being the appropriate response. Discuss the responses with the child. Ask the question, *"Which teddy is doing the right thing?"*. Example: one teddy falls over. The first teddy responds by laughing; the second teddy responds by showing concern and helping; the third teddy responds by turning and walking away. Teddies can be used to demonstrate other behaviours, such as snatching toys, being shouted at, being pushed/hit/nipped or being teased. Don't forget to use naturally occurring situations within the class to model appropriate responses.
Assessment	• Observe the child completing the activities. Offer praise and reward for success. • Use the Intervention Record Sheet to record evidence of progress.
Outcome	• The child recognises and responds to other children's feelings.
Resources	• Four teddies or dolls. • Intervention Record Sheet.

If the child continues to have significant difficulty in achieving a particular skill and evidence indicates they are making insufficient or no progress after four weeks of intervention you should consider consulting the school or setting SENDco.

The early years intervention activities 49

Personal, social and emotional development
Making relationships

The activities below are graded according to difficulty. Begin with the activity described in Step 1. Move on to the next step only when the child shows confidence and success. You may find that the child progresses through the first steps quickly. It is important to provide opportunities for the child to practice the activities daily.		**Card 32**

Observed behaviour	• Doesn't interact with other children.
Focus	• To develop social interaction.
Activity/ Strategy	To begin to show interest in other children. **Step 1** The adult puts photographs of three children into a bag. The child picks out a photograph of a girl or boy in the class. The adult names the girl or boy and suggests they go and find them to give them a toy. The adult gives the child a toy and together they go and find the girl or boy. When they find the girl or boy, the adult encourages the child to give them the toy. The level of support the adult gives will depend on the child's response. Initially you may have to model the whole process. Repeat the activity with the other photographs of other girls and boys. **Step 2** The adult puts photographs of three children in a bag. The child picks out a photograph of a girl or boy in the class. The adult names the girl or boy and suggests they go and find them to see what they are doing. Together they go and find the girl or boy and talk about what he or she is doing. **Step 3** Repeat Step 1. This time, encourage the child to do it independently. **Step 4** Repeat Step 2: support the child to stay and play.
Assessment	• Observe the child completing the activities. Offer praise and reward for success. • Use the Intervention Record Sheet to record evidence of progress.
Outcome	• The child begins to interact with other children.
Resources	• Photographs of children in the class. • Bag. • Toy. • Intervention Record Sheet.

If the child continues to have significant difficulty in achieving a particular skill and evidence indicates they are making insufficient or no progress after four weeks of intervention you should consider consulting the school or setting SENDco.

The early years intervention activities

Personal, social and emotional development
Making relationships

> The activities below are graded according to difficulty. Begin with the activity described in Step 1. Move on to the next step only when the child shows confidence and success. You may find that the child progresses through the first steps quickly. It is important to provide opportunities for the child to practice the activities daily. This will maximise their development and secure the memory of specific movements.

Card 33

Observed behaviour	- Inability to share and turn-take with other children.
Focus	- To develop-turn taking skills.
Activity/ Strategy	To turn-take and cooperate with others. **Step 1** The adult takes two similar toys. The child chooses one toy and the adult keeps the other. The child plays with their own toy for three minutes (use a sand timer that is visible to the child). The adult says, "*When the sand runs out you can play with my toy and I can play with your toy*". When the sand runs out, swap toys. Repeat two or three times. Introduce the word "swap" if appropriate. **Step 2** The child selects a favourite toy and the adult sits alongside the child. The child plays with the toy for one minute (use a sand timer that is visible to the child). The adult says to the child, "*When the sand runs out it will be my turn to play with the toy*". The adult models "*waiting*". When the sand runs out, the adult says, "*It is my turn now*". Turn the sand timer over and say to the child, "*When the sand runs out it will be your turn again*". Repeat the process and gradually extend the time. **Step 3** Invite a child to join in the activity. Repeat Steps 1 and 2. This is still a two-way turn-taking activity and the adult is supporting the process. **Step 4: The challenge** Incorporate the language of turn-taking.
Assessment	- Observe the child completing the activities. Offer praise and reward for success. - Use the Intervention Record Sheet to record evidence of progress.
Outcome	- The child is beginning to understand turn-taking.
Resources	- A selection of toys. - Sand timers for one and three minutes. - PSA Card 13. - Intervention Record Sheet.

If the child continues to have significant difficulty in achieving a particular skill and evidence indicates they are making insufficient or no progress after four weeks of intervention you should consider consulting the school or setting SENDco.

The early years intervention activities | 51

Personal, social and emotional development
Making relationships

The activities below are graded according to difficulty. Begin with the activity described in Step 1. Move on to the next step only when the child shows confidence and success. You may find that the child progresses through the first steps quickly. It is important to provide opportunities for the child to practice the activities daily. This will maximise their development and secure the memory of specific movements.		**Card 34**

Observed behaviour	• Inability to share and turn-take with other children.
Focus	• To develop the skill of sharing.
Activity/ Strategy	To share and cooperate with other children. **Step 1** Through observation, identify the area or the activity where sharing is an issue, e.g. the train set, cars, the creative area. **Step 2** Model sharing within the identified area or activity involving any children that are in the area. This is an adult-led activity. The adult counts out loud the number of trains and the number of children. The adult then shares out the train using the language of sharing and stress the outcome of sharing, e.g. "*We all have the same*". **Step 3** Repeat Step 2 but encourage the child with adult support to share out the trains to the other children. **Step 4** Within the classroom, provide regular opportunities for the child to share other toys and give out resources in small group times.
Assessment	• Observe the child completing the activities. Offer praise and reward for success. • Use the Intervention Record Sheet to record evidence of progress.
Outcome	• The child begins to demonstrate an understanding of sharing.
Resources	• The classroom environment. • PSA Card 13. • Intervention Record Sheet.

If the child continues to have significant difficulty in achieving a particular skill and evidence indicates they are making insufficient or no progress after four weeks of intervention you should consider consulting the school or setting SENDco.

52 The early years intervention activities

Personal, social and emotional development
Making relationships

The activities below are graded according to difficulty. Begin with the activity described in Step 1. Move on to the next step only when the child shows confidence and success. You may find that the child progresses through the first steps quickly. It is important to provide opportunities for the child to practice the activities daily. This will maximise their development and secure the memory of specific movements.	**Card 35**

Observed behaviour	• Demonstrates little self-control of own behaviour in conflict situations: 　o Aggression—hitting, biting, hair pulling. 　o Tantrums. 　o Runs away.
Focus	• To modify the child's behaviour.
Activity/ Strategy	To behave appropriately in conflict situations. Strategies to manage aggression: **Step 1** 1. Approach the conflict situation calmly. Intervene quickly and firmly to diffuse the situation, e.g. "*Tom stop, no hitting*". Engage another adult to apologise to the child (Sandi) who has experienced the "inappropriate behaviour". 2. Tom must be encouraged to move from the conflict area and not be made to apologise to Sandi as this could escalate the situation. 3. The other adult will continue to comfort Sandi and support them to continue their play. 4. Reinforce that the behaviour Tom has displayed is unacceptable. Use simple clear language, signs or gestures that his actions are inappropriate. For example, "*No hitting*". **Step 2** The adult will support Tom to re-engage in play, reinforcing the expected behaviour. For example, remind Tom, "*No hitting*". Use visual cues to reinforce, if necessary. Expect acknowledgment from Tom (thumbs up). Keep repeating Steps 1 and 2 until Tom's behaviour is modified. **Step 3** 1. When (and if) Sandi and Tom are willing, support the two children to engage in an activity together. 2. Offers specific praise "*I really like. . .*".
Assessment	• Observe the child in play with other children. Offer praise and reward for success. • Use the Intervention Record Sheet to record evidence of progress.
Outcome	• The child begins to demonstrate an understanding of acceptable and unacceptable behaviour.
Resources	• The classroom environment. • PSA Card 14. • Intervention Record Sheet.

If the child continues to have significant difficulty in achieving a particular skill and evidence indicates they are making insufficient or no progress after four weeks of intervention you should consider consulting the school or setting SENDco.

Personal, social and emotional development
Making relationships

The activities below are graded according to difficulty. Begin with the activity described in Step 1. Move on to the next step only when the child shows confidence and success. You may find that the child progresses through the first steps quickly. It is important to provide opportunities for the child to practice the activities daily. This will maximise their development and secure the memory of specific movements.	**Card 36**

Observed behaviour	• Finds it difficult to form relationships with children and or adults.
Focus	• To help the child form positive relationships.
Activity/ Strategy	To develop friendships with children and interact with adults. **Step 1** Through observation, identify the area or the activity where the child is most confident and comfortable. **Step 2** Show the child photographs of four children who also enjoy playing in the chosen area or enjoy the activity. Ask the child to name the children—give support if necessary. Tell the child, "*We are going to ask two children to join or play with us*". Support the child to select two children. Remember if you ask the child to select they may say "*NO*". **Step 3** Before inviting the children, decide on a play plan for that area or activity. For example, in the home corner they may decide to have a birthday party. Then talk together about what might happen. **Step 4** The adult encourages the chosen children to come and play. The adult remains in the area. They facilitate and support the children's play. Repeat Steps 1–4 daily in a range of situations. If the child's communication is limited, then visual strategies may need to be used.
Assessment	• Observe how the child's relationships develop. Offer praise and reward for success. • Use the Intervention Record Sheet to record evidence of progress.
Outcome	• The child begins to form relationships with children and adults.
Resources	• The classroom environment. • Photographs of children. • Intervention Record Sheet.

If the child continues to have significant difficulty in achieving a particular skill and evidence indicates they are making insufficient or no progress after four weeks of intervention you should consider consulting the school or setting SENDco.

Personal, social and emotional development self-confidence and self-awareness

Card 37

The strategies below are staged. Begin with the strategies described in Step 1. Move on to the next step only when the child shows confidence and success. You will find that each child will progress through this intervention at different rates. Some may become confident at separating from their parent/carer after Step 1 but others may require further steps.

Observed behaviour	• Difficulty separating from parents/carers.
Focus	• For the child to separate from parents/carers with increasing confidence.
Activity/ Strategy	To support the child to say goodbye to their parents/carers. **Step 1** The familiar adult meets the child and parent/carer as they arrive at the beginning of their day. The adult supports the parent/carer and child to take off the child's coat and hang it up, providing a running commentary on the process. The adult then asks the child to show and take his parent/carer to where they would like to play (it may be necessary to provide visual prompts). The adult plays alongside the parent/carer and child for ten minutes. The adult suggests in front of the child that the parent/carer goes for a cup of tea, while the adult and child continue to play together. Use a five-minute sand timer and explain to the child that when the sand runs out "mummy" will have finished her cup of tea and will be back. Once the parent/carer comes back into the classroom the child and the parent/carer go home (this teaches the child that when mummy comes back it is time to go home). Repeat daily gradually increasing the time separated from parent/carer to 20 minutes. Remember to comfort and reassure the child that "mummy" will be back soon. Once the child is happy and confident to be left for twenty minutes, move onto Step 2 if necessary. **Step 2** If necessary, the adult continues to meet and greet the child and parent/carer. The adult gives the child a choice of three jobs/activities to do (provide visual prompts). "Mummy" helps the child to choose the job/activity. The adult prompts the parent/carer to tell the child they are popping to the shops and will be back very soon (this having previously been arranged with the parent/carer). The child is encouraged to complete the job/activity and then if the child is settled they choose another job/activity. They may need reassurance that "mummy" will be back soon. Gradually extend the separation to an hour or more. **Step 3** Once the child separates confidently for the parent/carer, use the class visual timetable to reinforce the daily routine so that the child knows what is expected from them before the parent/carer comes to take them home.
Assessment	• Use the Intervention Record Sheet to record evidence of progress.
Outcome	• The child confidently separates from their parent/carer.
Resources	• Visual prompts. • Class visual timetable. • Intervention Record Sheet.

If the child continues to have significant difficulty in achieving a particular skill and evidence indicates they are making insufficient or no progress after four weeks of intervention you should consider consulting the school or setting SENDco.

The early years intervention activities · 55

Personal, social and emotional development self-confidence and self-awareness

The activities below are graded according to difficulty. Begin with the activity described in Step 1. Move on to the next step only when the child shows confidence and success. You may find that the child progresses through the first steps quickly. It is important to provide opportunities for the child to practice the activities daily.		**Card 38**

Observed behaviour	• Appears quiet, withdrawn and nervous.
Focus	• To begin to develop confident social interaction.
Activity/ Strategy	To develop interest, curiosity and confidence. **Step 1** The adult will go to where the child is and show them a multi-sensory toy/resource, e.g. a flashing ball. The adult plays with the ball and comments on the colours and sounds, etc. The adult then asks the child if they would like to play with it. This may encourage other children to approach. **Step 2** Repeat Step 1 using different resources each time and invite other children to join in the play. **Step 3** The adult asks the child to choose another child they would like to play with. The adult selects an appropriate turn-taking game and the adult and the two children sit in a quiet area of the room. The adult begins the game and models the language required for turn taking, e.g. "*Whose turn is it next*" or "*It's . . . turn next*". The adult and children play the game. **Step 4** The adult prepares the game for the two children but this time does not play with them. The adult reminds the children of the rules of the game and only intervenes when necessary to encourage communication between the two children.
Assessment	• Observe the child independently playing with another child. • Use the Intervention Record Sheet to record evidence of progress.
Outcome	• The child will seek other children to play with.
Resources	• A selection of multi-sensory resources and turn-taking activities. • Intervention Record Sheet.

If the child continues to have significant difficulty in achieving a particular skill and evidence indicates they are making insufficient or no progress after four weeks of intervention you should consider consulting the school or setting SENDco.

56 The early years intervention activities

Personal, social and emotional development self-confidence and self-awareness

	The following guidance is based on strategies rather than activities. It is important to be aware of what to avoid as well as how to support. Too much focus and pressure will not encourage the child to communicate.	**Card 39**

Observed behaviour	• Lacks confidence in speaking to adults and/or other children.
Focus	• To improve the child's confidence in talking.
Activity/ Strategy	**Always:** • Check that the child has no underlying speech difficulty by discreetly listening to parents or other children. • Allow time. Wait patiently for the child to respond. If the child is not willing to speak, ask them to show you what they want by looking or pointing to an object, activity or picture card. • Value the ways in which the child communicates. • Verbally confirm what the child is trying to communicate. **Never:** • Rush the child or show impatience. • Never make assumptions or choices for the child without giving them time and strategies to support their communication. **Activities** • Singing can develop confidence so provide plenty of opportunities for the child to sing. • Encourage the child to communicate through a toy or character of their choice. • Use their interests to facilitate comments, e.g. if they like cars, gently prompt the child to say something about them.
Assessment	• Observe the child, note their behaviour when they are talking either to their peers or adults. • Use the Intervention Record Sheet to record evidence of progress.
Outcome	• The child will develop more confidence in talking and make more attempts at speaking to adults and peers. **Note:** all adults, parents and other members of the family must be advised to follow the same advice at home.
Resources	• Activity and picture cards. • PSA Card 5. • Intervention Record Sheet.

If the child continues to have significant difficulty in achieving a particular skill and evidence indicates they are making insufficient or no progress after four weeks of intervention you should consider consulting the school or setting SENDco.

Personal, social and emotional development self-confidence and self-awareness

The activities below are graded according to difficulty. Begin with the activity described in Step 1. Move on to the next step only when the child shows confidence and success. You may find that the child progresses through the first steps quickly. It is important to provide opportunities for the child to practice the activities daily.		**Card 40**

Observed behaviour	• Needs support and encouragement to select activities independently.
Focus	• To make independent choices.
Activity/ Strategy	To use a personal planner independently. **Step 1** Before working with the child the adult makes a personal planner and a posting box (see example below in the Resources section). The adult shows the child five photographs or pictures that represent an activity within the classroom, e.g. a car. The adult asks the child to choose three favourite activities represented by the photographs/pictures. They then stick the photograph/pictures onto the squares on the planner. The adult will ask the child to look at the planner and choose where they want to play. When the child has finished playing in that area they can take the card that represents the activity off the planner and post it in the posting box. They are then asked to choose another activity. Repeat for the final activity on the planner. **Step 2** Provide the child with a planner with four or five boxes and a wider range of photographs/picture cards. **Step 3** Repeat Step 2. Encourage the child to use the planner independently.
Assessment	• Observe the child using their planner independently. • Use the Intervention Record Sheet to record evidence of progress.
Outcome	• The child will be able to choose activities independently.
Resources	• Two personal planning boards: one with three squares, the other with four or five squares with a strip of Velcro in the middle of each square. • A set of photograph/picture cards of classroom activities with Velcro on the back. • A "posting box", e.g. a shoe box covered in paper and a slit cut into the lid. • PSA Card 15. • Intervention Record Sheet.

If the child continues to have significant difficulty in achieving a particular skill and evidence indicates they are making insufficient or no progress after four weeks of intervention you should consider consulting the school or setting SENDco.

58 The early years intervention activities

Personal, social and emotional development self-confidence and self-awareness

		Card 41
The activities below are graded according to difficulty. Begin with the activity described in Step 1. Move on to the next step only when the child shows confidence and success. You may find that the child progresses through the first steps quickly. It is important to provide opportunities for the child to practice the activities daily.		

Observed behaviour	• Has predictable routines, always plays in the same areas, is reluctant to try new activities or "have a go" with different resources.
Focus	• To begin to show interest in other activities and resources.
Activity/ Strategy	To begin to play in other areas of the classroom. **Step 1** Before working with the child the adult makes a personal planner (with two squares) and a posting box (see example below in the Resources section). The adult shows the child three photographs or pictures that represent an activity within the classroom, e.g. a car. Include one activity that they are familiar with. The adult asks the child to choose two activities represented by the photographs/pictures. They then put the photographs/pictures in the boxes on the planner. The adult will ask the child to look at the planner and choose where they want to play. Together they go to the activity and the adult models play and encourages the child to use the resources. When the play has come to a natural end the child can take the card that represents the activity they have completed off the planner and post it in the posting box. The child is then asked to go to the next activity, playing alongside the adult. When the play has come to a natural end the child can take the card that represents the activity they have completed off the planner and post it in the posting box. **Step 2** Repeat Step 1. Use a personal planner with three squares. Extend the number of photograph/picture cards to four.
Assessment	• Use the Intervention Record Sheet to record evidence of progress.
Outcome	• The child will be able to choose an activity, stay and play.
Resources	• Personal planning board with three squares, each box with a strip of Velcro in the middle of each box. • A set of photograph/picture cards of classroom activities with Velcro on the back. • A "posting box", e.g. a shoe box covered in paper and a slit cut into the lid. • PSA Card 16. • Intervention Record Sheet.

If the child continues to have significant difficulty in achieving a particular skill and evidence indicates they are making insufficient or no progress after four weeks of intervention you should consider consulting the school or setting SENDco.

The early years intervention activities 59

Personal, social and emotional development managing feelings and behaviour

The strategies below are intended to support practitioners to confidently manage children's feelings and behaviours. This is an inclusive approach to managing a range of behaviours that children may present. It is important that the strategies are consistently implemented by all adults who have contact with the child.		**Card 42**

Observed behaviour	• Is unaware of the consequences of their own behaviour. • Responds inappropriately when others are upset or hurt. • Finds difficulty in adapting their behaviour in different situations. • Shows a lack of awareness of the boundaries and expectations within the setting. • Has difficulty in coping with "change".
Focus	• To support children to respond appropriately to routines and expectations in the learning environment.
Strategies	**Provide a visual environment that doesn't over-stimulate children's senses:** • Avoid creating areas where children cannot be seen. • Maintain quiet, tidy, organised, light and airy learning areas. • Use muted colours for displays, try to avoid overcrowding the walls and keep hanging displays to a minimum. • Ensure children can move easily around the classroom space. **Reinforce routines:** • Provide and refer regularly to the class visual timetable using a bead on a string under the timetable to show the passing of time. Use the timetable at times of all transitions. • Provide an individual daily timetable for children who find it particularly difficult to cope with changes in routines and activities. Encourage the child to use the timetable. For example, when the child completes an activity, a card is removed from the timetable and posted in a box or placed in a "finished tray". **Reinforce expectations:** • Clearly establish what you expect children to do in all areas of the learning environment. Display visual prompts in all areas, for example *sharing*, *walking*, *tidying up*, *being kind* and *friendly*. • Adults should remind children of the expected behaviour by using portable visual prompts to reinforce expected behaviour. • Always communicate in a clear, simple and visual way. Refer to the Supporting Communication cards (Intervention Activities 16 and 17, pp 33, 34).
Assessment	• Observe the child or children following routines and expectations. • Use the Intervention Record Sheet to record evidence of progress.
Outcome	The child is beginning to respond appropriately to boundaries and expectations and adapt their behaviour.
Resources	• A selection of visual prompts and symbols. • Visual timetables. • PSA Card 16. • Intervention Record Sheet.

Personal, social and emotional development managing feelings and behaviour

Card 43

The strategies below are intended to support practitioners to confidently manage children's feelings and behaviours. This is an inclusive approach to managing a range of behaviours that children may present. It is important that the strategies are consistently implemented by all adults who have contact with the child.

Observed behaviour	- Is unaware of the consequences of their own behaviour. - Responds inappropriately when others are upset or hurt. - Finds difficulty in adapting their behaviour in different situations. - Shows a lack of awareness of the boundaries and expectations within the setting. - Has difficulty in coping with "change".
Focus	- To support children to respond appropriately to adults and children.
Strategies	**Through role play and the daily routine, either with a child or an adult, model the following behaviours:** - Sharing. - Turn-taking. - Good manners. - Kindness. - Helpfulness. - Cooperation. **Modification of inappropriate low-level behavior:** - Some low-level behaviours are best ignored, particularly if the child or other children are not in danger. - For more persistent low-level behaviour, praise the child when they least expect it, i.e. "catch them being good". Try to avoid waiting for the child to display inappropriate behaviour. It is important initially to overload the child with praise for the behaviour you expect. - If a child displays inappropriate behaviour, then use "proximity praise". For example, Tommy is lying on the carpet and not sitting up during story time. Praise the children beside Tommy who are sitting appropriately. Use this strategy consistently. - Constantly remind the child of the behaviour you expect, e.g. "*Tommy, remember to sit, not lie on the carpet*". **Modification of inappropriate high-level behaviour:** - High-level behaviours should not be ignored and may require action. - For aggressive behavior, such as hitting, biting, pushing, etc., the adult should respond immediately. Show a hand signal "stop" or a firm verbal "*No*" accompanied by a clearly displeased facial expression. If the behaviour is repeated, then take the child away to another area to play and reinforce the expected behavior, e.g. '*No hitting*'. Observe their play and catch them being good. Should the inappropriate behaviour continue, then 'Time Away' should be introduced in the following way: **Step 1.** Remove the child from the situation to another area or a designated space. **Step 2.** Remind the child of the behaviour they have to change, e.g. "*No hitting*." **Step 3.** The adult stays with the child for an agreed amount of time (you may wish to use a sand timer). **Step 4.** The adult will then accompany the child to an area of the adult's choosing and model appropriate play and interaction with other children.

The early years intervention activities

	Managing the extremes: When children display extreme behaviour, it must be dealt with immediately. The child will often be highly distressed. The following strategies could be implemented: **Step 1.** Attempt to lead the child out of the area. **Step 2.** If the child refuses to go, then remove the other children from that area. **Step 3.** Assess the risks and remove any dangers, e.g. toys, shoes, mobile objects, etc. **Step 4.** Place a cushion or a soft, fleecy blanket close to the child to offer sensory comfort. Allow the child time to calm down. The adult should not speak to the child at this point. The adult should avoid any physical contact with the child. **Step 5.** When the child is calmer, offer them a drink and/or some therapeutic toys, e.g. a rain stick, glitter stick or something similar. **Things to avoid:** - Too much language: keep it simple and precise. - Carrying a child.
Assessment	- Observe the child or children following routines and expectations. - Use the Intervention Record Sheet to record evidence of progress.
Outcome	- The child is beginning to respond appropriately to boundaries and expectations and adapt their behaviour.
Resources	- A selection of visual prompts and symbols. - Visual timetables. - PSA Card 16. - Intervention Record Sheet.

The early years intervention activities

Personal, social and emotional development managing feelings and behaviour

		Card 44
Personal, social and emotional development are three building blocks of life. Children need to have a sense of who they are, how to form relationships and understand and manage their feelings and emotions if they are to become life-long learners.		

Observed behaviour	• Is unable to show an understanding of their emotions. • Responds inappropriately when others are upset.
Focus	To develop supportive, inclusive teaching strategies in order to help the child to begin to accept the needs of others and become aware of their own emotions.
Activity/ Strategy	• Name and talk about a wide range of feelings with the child. • Use "feelings" cards to help describe emotions. • The adult models how to manage feelings, e.g. anger, sadness, happiness, etc. • Use books, puppets, stories and persona dolls to help the child consider feelings. • Use a "feelings frame" with pictures of different emotions, e.g. *crying, laughing, smiling*, etc. and teach children to show how they are feeling by putting a sticker beside the feeling that best describes how they are feeling. • Plan a circle time session where the child can recall when they felt different emotions, e.g. when were they last happy or sad, excited or bored, etc.
Assessment	• Observe how children respond to the strategies and begin to use them. • Use the Intervention Record Sheet to record evidence of progress.
Outcome	• Children will begin to respond to their own and other's feelings.
Resources	• Photographs. • Feelings frame. • Persona dolls. • Puppets. • Stories. • Intervention Record Sheet.

6 Parents as partners

When considering working with parents or carers, it is important to get this right from the very start. From time to time practitioners will identify children as having some difficulties or delays in their learning and it might be necessary to raise concerns with parents. When talking to parents or carers, practitioners must have absolute confidence that a barrier to learning has been identified. It is essential to find out just what is stopping those children accessing the curriculum. Regardless of whether it is the Foundation Stage, Key Stage One or Key Stage Two curriculum, it is really important that we find out why the children have any sort of delay. The best early identification tends to happen in the Early Years because practitioners routinely look closely at child development as soon as they begin attending. It is possible to pick up issues across the age ranges, but it is best for it to take place in the Early Years whenever possible to prevent the situation becoming much worse.

There will always be a period when children first start school when allowances are made for settling in—a sort of "catch up" period. What is important to avoid is allowing this "they'll catch up" period to be too long because some children may never catch up. They may never close the gap in differences between themselves and their peers. **The earlier practitioners can respond to this, the better!** When delays are identified, it is very important to take the time to investigate what may be the cause(s) and a sensitive approach to parents is essential.

Behavioural issues are often a sign that there may be an underlying delay in a child's development. These can be diagnosed and dealt with whilst the child is in their school or Early Years setting—including a childminding provision—but sometimes it is useful or even necessary to enlist the help and support of parents and carers. Behaviour can be a very difficult area to discuss with parents. Initially it will be necessary to sensitively approach the parents and invite them to have a chat so that concerns about their child can be conveyed. This will be the same, whether the child is in the Early Years, Key Stage One or Two.

Often, the easiest time to approach parents is in the school yard, when they are dropping off in the morning or collecting their child at the end of the day/session. It is not unusual to see teachers going into the yard after school and saying something like, "Mrs. Smith, could I have a word?" and beckoning them to come across. Consider this from that parent's point of view. Imagine that you are the parent in this scenario. You might feel singled out or maybe embarrassed. Just the intonation of ". . . could I have a word?" can create a barrier from the start. You might be conscious of the fact that other parents can hear the summons. You might be fearful that other parents will be forming an opinion that your child is troublesome and not well behaved. You might

DOI: 10.4324/9781003243298-6

64 Parents as partners

fear that other parents may become judgmental of your parenting skills or they might want to keep their children away from your child.

Be very mindful when approaching parents or carers. Rather than confronting them publicly in the school yard, perhaps consider communicating with them via telephone earlier on in the day, asking if it would be possible to meet to have a little chat. This may not put them completely at ease, but at least it will be possible to arrange a meeting without raising unnecessary fears in the mind of the parent.

This very first meeting should focus on the behaviour of the child in the first instance and what may have been the cause. It should ALWAYS be the behaviour itself that is the focus of the conversation. The child's behaviour might be undesirable, but it might just be "different" from the norm. No parent wants to be told that their child is misbehaving or is "different", but at some point, it must be addressed. It is essential to have a high degree of sensitivity when giving advice to parents. Set the scene. Meet in a calm, quiet and private place. Have tissues at the ready—offer a cup of tea or coffee. This way you can start to talk about your concerns about their child in a relaxed manner. Be reassuring that what you are saying may not necessarily mean that the child will not go on to be successful. It just means that you and the parents need to work together to find a successful solution to the problem. Try and identify and remove or reduce whatever barriers or delays may be discovered. You can then act positively and can put robust interventions in place, reassuring the parents that everything is being done to help the child.

Always keep your language simple and uncomplicated, try to avoid jargon or acronyms and specialist language that they may not understand. Talk sensitively to the parents, without pressure, about what they might do to help at home and how you and they might be able to work together to help the child. At all costs, try to avoid making the parent feel guilty if they are unable to offer the support you are asking for. They may already have a feeling of guilt over their child and blame themselves for the delay or difference. If the parents are willing to help and support you, make sure that anything you ask of them is fun and easy. With supportive, meaningful, systematic intervention, the child is more likely to improve.

There may be occasions where a child may not make the expected progress, despite a period of systematic intervention. In such a case, it may be appropriate to discuss with the parents the next level of intervention or possible further assessment. Having now, hopefully, developed a good relationship with the parents or carers, you will have eased them into considering that there may be something of greater concern, which may require the involvement of the school/setting SENDCo.

There is a wonderful analogy called "Going to Holland" which is powerful in helping parents face difficult situations. The story describes a family planning to go on a holiday to a Caribbean island, but when they arrive at the airport, they discover that the flight has been cancelled. They are no longer able to go, but they have been offered an alternative holiday to Holland. They are very disappointed and really sad about it, thinking that this was not the holiday they wanted. This was not what they expected, but they really do not have a choice. They have already packed their suitcases and they are standing in the airport, so they decide to go with the offer. When they get to Holland, they start exploring and looking at what Holland has to offer. They go to see the fields of tulips, the windmills and many wonderful places they never knew about. They realise that going to Holland wasn't so bad after all. Things were quite pleasant, even fun and they *could* have a successful, happy holiday, despite the unexpected change of destination.

Consider a parent's expectation of having a child and wanting the brightest future for them and then all of a sudden, unexpectedly, somebody tells them that they have a "*concern*". As soon as the words "*concern*" or "*I'm worried . . .*" are used, it can hit them like a ton of bricks. All of a sudden, their journey into life with their child has potentially changed—*even if it is only a slight concern*. This provides the practitioner with the opportunity to guide them through a process. It can be done in a very positive way. It is possible to explain that "*It doesn't mean 'this' and it certainly **doesn't** mean 'that' but if it did . . .*" then they would be supported throughout the journey. There will be expectations on the way. There will be professionals on the way to guide them throughout the process and it will not be so bad.

Think again of the holiday analogy: acknowledging the disappointment of not going on the desired holiday, compared to going on a different journey that will prove to be just as enjoyable and successful, albeit slightly different. This can help get across a powerful message. Getting parents on board but not demanding that they must do "this" or "that" with their children requires gentle encouragement. If parents can say "*Gosh, this is fun . . .*" instead of avoiding supporting the child because it isn't fun, this is a much better way of engaging parents. It is important to guide them through experiences that are going to be very positive. Parents should be encouraged not to have **overly** high expectations of their child. High expectations are good! We all have high expectations of our children and for parents who have just been told that perhaps their expectations won't be met, using explanations such as "*. . . well, it might not be the same or slightly different . . . . but they can still be successful in whatever they do . . .*" can be very encouraging. When working with parents, practitioners need to be very sensitive. If you get it wrong, it can have quite devastating consequences for a family. It is all about that early nurture. Parents need to be supported and nurtured into feeling confident with how you are dealing with their child, comfortable with what is going to happen in the future and to be guided through procedures with which they may be unfamiliar. Instil in them the confidence that they can engage in, understand, and support the work you are doing with their child.

When you have your parent evenings or when you are meeting a parent or carer for the first time, remember to have regard for some of these suggestions. You may be a parent yourself and maybe have had a similar experience. Think about the last time when you felt anxious or in an unfamiliar situation. It might be when you first went to see the bank manager or doctor to ask them a question. The feelings you experienced sitting in the waiting room and anticipating the response—that you are going to get a "*yes*" or "*no*" even if you are just applying to borrow some money. Is it a "*yes*" or "*no*" if you are waiting to find out whether or not you have a certain medical condition.

Always remember to consider the possible anxiety and stress of the moment when you invite a parent in; how you invite them in makes all the difference. Will it be, "*Mrs. Smith, could I see you for a moment*", or "*Dear Mr. and Mrs. Smith, would it be possible for you to pop in and have a little chat about Samantha . . .?*" From then on, that parent is going to feel anxious, so please get it right! It is so important.

Practitioners may want to encourage parents to use the Parent Support Activities (PSA) at home to support what is taking place in the setting. The following Parent

Parents as partners

Support Activity cards can be copied or downloaded and then given to parents or carers. Pictures accompanying the activities can also be downloaded and printed out to help support the activities at home. Some parents will be more than happy to carry out the activities with their child. Bear in mind, however, that for some parents, following a list of instructions for activities may be off-putting. Be sensitive as to what you perceive parents are willing or able to attempt. You may want to give careful thought as to how to encourage parents or carers to get involved. It may be just as well to describe the activity or try to make it into a game that can be done at home.

7 Parent support activities (PSA)

Parent Support Activity (PSA) Card User Guide

PSA Toolkit	EYI
SPEECH, LANGUAGE and COMMUNICATION	
Card 1 Limited speech	1
Card 2 Difficulty speaking clearly	3
Card 3 Difficulty with attention and listening	11
Card 4 Inability to sit still	13
Card 5 Not understanding or responding to adults	10, 39
PHYSICAL DEVELOPMENT, HEALTH and SELF CARE	
Card 6 Tripping, falling and bumping	18, 19, 20, 21
Card 7 Difficulty holding a pencil	24
Card 8 Difficulty with cutting	25
Card 9 Difficulty riding a bike	22
Card 10 Excessive salivation	4, 29
Card 11 Toilet training	
Card 12 Getting dressed	28
PERSONAL, SOCIAL and EMOTIONAL	
Card 13 Difficulty sharing and taking turns	33, 34
Card 14 Aggressive behaviour	35
Card 15 Finding it hard to make choices	40
Card 16 Not doing as they are asked	41, 42, 43

DOI: 10.4324/9781003243298-7

68 Parent support activities (PSA)

These cards are available online to download along with:

- Letter sound cards
- Activity cards
- Object cards

Go to www.routledge.com/cw/speechmark and click on the cover of this book. Click the 'Sign in or Request Access' button and follow the instructions in order to access the resources.

SPEECH, LANGUAGE and COMMUNICATION

PSA 1 *Limited speech*

What am I seeing?

My child does not speak much.
When my child speaks it is hard to understand what they are saying. My child often shows frustration or anger towards adults and friends and sometimes gets upset.

What might this mean?

There may be several reasons why your child has not developed speech or cannot be understood, e.g. hearing difficulty (VERY common), delayed speech development or physical disorder.

What do I want to make better?

To help my child communicate better with adults and children even though speech has not yet fully developed.

What do I need?

You will need some pictures or photos and matching objects of familiar objects or toys and activities (see below).
A lanyard or key ring.

What could I try?

Whilst waiting for a hearing assessment and/or a speech therapy appointment, consider trying the following to help your child communicate successfully with others:

- Use the six picture cards of objects, e.g. teddy bear, building brick, pencil, toothbrush along with the real objects.
- Ask your child to choose a picture card and show it to you. Give the child the object that matches the picture—this is called "Picture Exchange".
- Use the six activity cards or photos, e.g. playing in the sand, drinking milk, putting coat on, doing jigsaw puzzle, playing with a train set.
- Ask your child to choose an activity card that shows what *they* want to do and show it to you. Carry out the activity your child has chosen. Have fun carrying out the activity.
- Encourage your child to use pictures or photos to tell or show you what they want to say or do. You may want to provide more pictures to help them communicate what they want to do or say.

- Model the speaking whilst exchanging the picture or photos and encourage the child to use their own words.

What will I see if I do this?

If you encourage your child to use non-verbal communication, e.g. point to or select something, you will begin to see a happier child who shows more confidence in getting their message across to you. You are likely to see less frustration and see better behaviour.

What will I do if I don't see an improvement in my child's ability to speak or communicate?

Ask yourself these questions:

- Have I asked everyone in the home to use the "picture exchange" to help your child communicate?
- Have I explained everything clearly to my child and am I certain they understand?
- Do I have enough pictures or photos for my child to use?
- Am I allowing my child enough time to show me what they need?

What else could I do?

- It is important to have their hearing checked as this is a common cause of speech not developing. Refer to your health visitor or visit your GP and ask for a hearing assessment as soon as possible along with a referral to a speech therapist.
- Share what you have done with your child's nursery or school.

PSA 2 Difficulty speaking clearly

What am I seeing?

My child is not able to produce clear sounds and words. They often miss the beginning or end sounds of words, e.g. "b" for bus or "og" for dog. Sometimes both are missing, or they say a different sound, e.g. "tar" for car.

What might this mean?

This may be directly linked to hearing loss; therefore, your child might need to be referred for a hearing assessment. This may also indicate a need for a specialist speech and language therapy assessment.

What do I want to make better?

To help my child to produce clearer sounds and words.

What do I need?

You will need a set of picture cards (of everyday objects—your nursery or Reception teacher will be able to provide you with these), letter sound cards and a mirror.

What could I try?

Start by providing a quiet/noise-free environment:

- Ask your child to sit beside you.
- Start with the individual sound card and ask your child to try and say the sound. Make a note of the sounds the child does not say accurately or finds tricky.
- Don't correct mispronunciation in a negative manner. Repeat the word back to them with the correct pronunciation.
- Work through the tricky sounds one by one. Try to use actions to go with some of the sounds, e.g. for the sound "m" rub your tummy and say "mmm".
- Always model the short sound of a letter, e.g. "a", as in "ant" and not "ay" as in "ace". Avoid adding an "uh" sound to the end of sounds such as l, n, m, r, s, etc. Say "lll" not "luh"; "rrr" not ruh; "sss" not "suh".
- Ask your child to copy you and look in a mirror so they can see themselves making the sounds.
- Some sounds are made from the back of the mouth and are difficult to model and explain (e.g. "k", "G"), so begin with the sounds where the mouth shape is obvious and easy to copy (e.g. mmm, sss, fff, thhh).
- Repeat this activity for two minutes every day in a quiet room.
- Eventually add some background noise and continue to repeat the activity.

Parent support activities (PSA)

What will I see if I do this?

Your child will gradually begin to say a greater number of sounds much more clearly.

What will I do if I don't see an improvement?

Ask yourself these questions:

- Am I modelling the sounds clearly to my child?
- Am I certain they can hear them?

What else could I do?

- If your child uses a dummy, it should be removed when they speak. Dummies should only be used to pacify very young children (if at all) and be taken away completely as soon as possible.
- Sing songs and say nursery rhymes.
- Record the sounds your child says on your phone or other recording device and let them hear the difference between your sounds and theirs.
- Refer to a health visitor or speech and language therapist.
- Share what you have done with your child's nursery or school.

PSA 3 Difficulty with attention and listening

What am I seeing?

My child rarely looks at me when I speak. They rarely respond straight away when I or other people say "hello", "goodbye" or say something else.

What might this mean?

When children avoid eye contact and look as if they are not listening, there may be a number of reasons. Good listening and attention require good eye contact which should improve listening skills.

What do I want to make better?

To encourage my child to stop, look and listen.

What do I need?

You will need a hand signal or "stop" sign, e.g. a hand picture (palm facing forward).

What could I try?

- Begin in a quiet environment (make sure the TV is switched off).
- When you want your child to look and listen, approach the child and say their name. Ask them to stop what they are doing using a calm, clear voice.
- It may be necessary to first join in with their activity and then get their attention. Concentrate on one thing—sharing the child's interest.
- Ask your child to look at you or move into their line of sight.
- Only when your child is looking at you, say what you want to say to them.
- You may need to use the "stop" signal if your child still does not respond.
- Encourage your child to respond and do what you have said.
- Repeat this regularly.
- When your child is used to stopping and looking at you, begin to give your child a simple instruction.
- Continue to do this each time you want your child to listen to you. Try to avoid speaking until your child looks at you.
- Try this in a noisier environment.

What will I see if I do this?

- Your child will learn to stop when their name is called then listen more carefully and follow your instructions. Your child's listening and attention skills will improve. If they stop and look at you, their willingness to carry out a request or greet you will improve.

Parent support activities (PSA)

What will I do if I don't see an improvement?

Ask yourself these questions:

- Am I being firm enough when I ask my child to stop and look?
- Do I do this every time I want to speak to my child?
- Do other familiar adults do the same?
- Does my child find giving eye contact difficult?
- Is your child hearing their name being called?
- What distractions are there?

What else could I do?

- Discuss your concerns with your health visitor, your child's nursery or school.
- Have your child's hearing checked.

PSA 4 Inability to sit still

What am I seeing?

My child is unable to sit still either on a chair or on the carpet. They often fiddle with things and fidget. They are very easily distracted. I can't get them to concentrate on anything for more than a few seconds.

What might this mean?

There may be several reasons why your child has not developed the skill of sitting and paying attention. It could be that they do not have good control of movement and/or coordination or that the activity you want them to pay attention to is not easy to understand or hear.

What do I want to make better?

To help my child to sit still and pay attention.

What do I need?

You will need a heavy object such as a large book or a small bag of potatoes and a timer (sand-, egg-, phone app). A toy the child can fiddle with or some play dough/plasticine/Blu Tack®.

What could I try?

Let's start with helping your child's control of movement:

- Ask your child to sit on the carpet to share a book with you.
- Make sure they are in a supported, comfortable position, e.g. resting their back against a wall or sofa with their legs stretched out in front of them (this may be all your child needs to help them sit still).
- Offer your child a heavy object to place on their knees whilst they are listening to a story or watching a short TV programme. The weight on their legs makes it easier for them to sit still.
- You might want to give your child a fiddle toy.
- Share a book and ask your child to try and sit still for three minutes. Use the timer (which they should be able to see).
- You may want to ask your child to sit for longer periods of time and with lighter or no weights. Remove any distractions.

What will I see if I do this?

If you encourage your child to do some or all of these things whilst sitting, you are likely to see an improvement in the length of time they are able to sit. Your child will begin to be able to control their movement if weights are used. This will also improve their attention and concentration skills.

What will I do if I don't see an improvement in my child's movement and attention and concentration?

Ask yourself these questions:

- Have I explained everything clearly to my child and am I certain they understand?
- Does the book I am sharing with my child interest them?
- Do I have the right weighted object? Ask your child to choose.
- Am I allowing my child enough time to get used to sitting with a weighted object on their legs?

What else could I do?

- Check your child's other movement skills and coordination.
- Check your child's understanding of language, i.e. do they understand the words you use in your instructions?
- Share what you have done with your child's nursery or school.

PSA 5 Not understanding or responding to adults

What am I seeing?

My child often ignores me, does not seem to understand what I am saying and doesn't respond in the right way when I ask them to do something.
My child often looks at me blankly and gets cross with me.

What might this mean?

This is an area of communication and language that can often be overlooked. If your child appears to be ignoring you or carrying on with what they are doing even if you have asked them to do something else, then they may have a difficulty with understanding your choice of words or they may have a low level of hearing. They may need some visual support.

What do I want to make better?

To help my child understand and follow my instructions.

What do I need?

A range of "daily routine" cards, photos or prompts (your nursery or Reception teacher will be able to provide you with these) to help your child understand what you are saying. For example, select pictures of a coat, shoes, bath time, teatime, tidy up, anything that you feel is important to you and your child.

What could I try?

To help your child understand others, consider trying the following:

- Select a range of picture cards or photographs to help your child understand what you are saying.
- Keep your language very clear and simple. Use single words if necessary.
- Try not to assume that your child understands everything you say.
- Use large, clear pictures to get messages across to your child more quickly.
- Use hand gestures (miming "*drink*", "*brush*", etc.) to help get your messages across.

What will I see if I do this?

If you encourage your child to get used to visual support, you will begin to see a happier child who shows more confidence in doing the right thing for you and others. You are likely to see less anger and frustration.

Parent support activities (PSA)

What will I do if I don't see an improvement in my child's communication?

Ask yourself these questions:

- Have I asked everyone in the household to do the same to help my child communicate?
- Am I using a wide enough range of picture cards and prompts to help my child understand?
- Am I allowing my child enough time to work out what I am saying?

What else could I do?

- Consider arranging a hearing assessment and possibly a referral for speech and language therapy via your GP or health visitor.
- Discuss your concerns with your child's key worker or teacher.

PHYSICAL DEVELOPMENT, HEALTH and SELF CARE

PSA 6 *Tripping, falling and bumping*

What am I seeing?

My child often trips and falls over things. They walk a little awkwardly and prefer to run rather than walk.

What do I want to make better?

To improve my child's balance and coordination.

What things do I need?

You will need some masking tape.

What could I try?

- Help your child to slow their movements down so that they have more controlled movements.
- Design a straight pathway (either indoors or outdoors) using masking tape. Make it about three meters in length and, to begin with, about thirty centimetres apart.
- Ask your child to walk between the lines. Encourage them to stay on the pathway, keeping their feet between the two strips of tape.
- Offer your child some help if they need it.
- When the child is confident and can walk easily between the lines independently, ask them to walk backwards along the pathway between the lines. Again, help might be needed at this stage.
- Eventually reduce the width of the pathway.
- If this is improving your child's movement then consider creating a curved pathway (make it into an adventure).

What will I see if I do all these things?

If you follow the suggestions regularly and repeatedly, your child will begin to walk with more controlled movements, and you may not see so much tripping and falling. They will have learned to slow down their movements.

Parent support activities (PSA)

What will I do if I don't see an improvement?

Ask yourself these questions:

- Have I been clear about what I expect from my child?
- Have I explained everything clearly?
- Am I doing this at least once a day with my child?
- Have you spotted signs of other gross or fine motor coordination difficulties, e.g. holding a pencil, picking up tiny objects, dressing, jumping, hopping, riding a bike, etc.?

What else could I do?

- If you are concerned about your child's movement or coordination, then perhaps consider a referral to an occupational therapist via your GP or school.
- Discuss your concerns with your health visitor, your child's key worker at nursery or teacher at school.

PSA 7 *Difficulty holding a pencil*

What am I seeing?

My child is not able to hold a pencil properly. They grip it in their palm and not between finger and thumb.

What do I want to make better?

To improve my child's pencil grip so that they can learn to mark-make or write more successfully.

What things do I need?

- Finger fun area: bubble wrap, play dough, jars with screw tops, pegs and washing line and cotton reels, nuts and bolts etc.
- You will also need ten cotton balls, large and small plastic tweezers or tongs, raisins, dried peas and a container.

What could I try?

Daily exercises will help to tighten wrist and finger muscles and develop good coordination.

- Create a "finger fun" area with the resources listed above.
- Ask your child to explore the "finger fun" area at least once a day. Show your child how to use the resources, e.g. pop bubble wrap between finger and thumb, screw lids off jars and back on again, peg pieces of paper onto a washing line, thread cotton reels onto a piece of washing line, etc.
- Show your child how to hold tweezers or tongs correctly between thumb and finger to pick up the cotton balls and transfer them into a container.
- Do this regularly then ask your child to swap to using small tweezers to pick up raisins.
- Once your child can pick up raisins with tweezers ask them to pick them up between their finger and thumb.
- Help your child to practice picking up a range of small objects and hold them between their finger and thumb whilst you count to twenty before they place the objects into a container.
- Show your child how to hold a pencil correctly between finger and thumb alongside doing all the above exercises (refer to the picture provided by your child's nursery or Reception teacher). Practice every day!

What will I see if I do all these things?

If you follow the suggestions regularly and repeatedly, your child's fine motor coordination will improve. They will soon be able to hold a pencil correctly.

What will I do if I don't see an improvement?

Ask yourself these questions:

- Have I been clear about what I expect from my child?
- Have I explained everything clearly?
- Am I doing this at least once a day with my child?
- Look for signs of other gross or fine motor coordination difficulties, e.g. picking up tiny objects, dressing, jumping, hopping, riding a bike, etc.

What else could I do?

- If you are concerned about your child's movement or coordination, then perhaps consider a referral to an occupational therapist via your GP or school.
- Discuss your concerns with your health visitor, your child's key worker at nursery or teacher at school.

PSA 8 Difficulty with cutting

What am I seeing?

My child is not able to use scissors and finds difficulty cutting. They cannot hold the scissors correctly.

What do I want to make better?

To improve my child's fine motor skills so that they can use scissors properly.

What things do I need?

You will need a pair of spring-loaded or double-handed scissors, play dough and paper strips to snip and cut.

10 x cotton balls. Large plastic tweezers or tongs, raisins, dried peas and a container.

For finger exercising, collect bubble wrap, play dough, jars with screw tops, pegs and washing line and cotton reels, nuts and bolts, etc.

What could I try?

Daily exercises will help to tighten wrist and finger muscles and develop good coordination:

- Give the child a long paper straw or some thin strips of paper. Show your child how to hold the sprung scissors and how to snip the straw and paper into small pieces.
- Ask your child to roll the play dough into a long, thin sausage shape then show them how to snip the dough into small pieces.
- When your child can snip successfully with the scissors they have chosen, draw a straight line onto a piece of paper with a thick-felt tip pen. Ask your child to cut along the line.
- Next, draw curved lines for your child to cut along.
- Encourage your child to do this every day until they can begin to cut shapes.
- Create a "finger fun" area with the resources listed above.
- Ask your child to explore the "finger fun" area at least once a day. Show your child how to use the resources, e.g. pop bubble wrap between finger and thumb, screw lids off jars and back on again, peg pieces of paper onto a washing line.
- Show your child how to hold tweezers or tongs correctly between thumb and finger to pick up the cotton balls and transfer them into a container.
- Do this regularly then ask your child to swap to using small tweezers to pick up raisins.
- Once your child can pick up raisins with tweezers ask them to pick them up between their finger and thumb.
- Help your child to practice picking up a range of small objects and hold them between their finger and thumb whilst you count to twenty before they place the objects into a container.

- Show your child how to hold a pencil correctly between finger and thumb alongside doing all the above exercises (see picture included with Letter Sound Cards—these can be provided by your child's nursery or Reception). Practice every day.

What will I see if I do all these things?

If you follow the suggestions regularly and repeatedly, your child will be able to use scissors more successfully for cutting. Fine motor coordination will improve.

What will I do if I don't see an improvement?

Ask yourself these questions:

- Have I been clear about what I expect from my child?
- Have I explained everything clearly?
- Am I doing this at least once a day with my child?

Look for signs of other gross or fine motor coordination difficulties, e.g. holding a pencil, picking up tiny objects, dressing, jumping, hopping, riding a bike, etc.

What else could I do?

- If you are concerned about your child's movement or coordination, then perhaps consider a referral to an occupational therapist via your GP, health visitor or school.
- Discuss your concerns with your child's key worker at nursery or teacher at school.

Parent support activities (PSA)   **85**

PSA 9 Difficulty riding a bike

What am I seeing?

My child can't seem to learn to ride a bike. They have difficulty pedalling.

What do I want to make better?

To improve my child's coordination so that they can ride a bike confidently.

What things do I need?

You will need a play tunnel, large cardboard boxes, blankets, paper fish, a chair, sheets of paper or something that the child can step on and use as stepping stones.

What could I try?

For good coordination, your child needs their arms and legs to work either in combination or in opposition. Crawling is very important.

- Encourage your child to creep and crawl.
- Provide a play tunnel for your child to crawl through every day. This could be the entrance to their bedroom.
- Large cardboard boxes, tables and chairs covered with blankets can be used to crawl under.
- Play blowfish with the paper fish. Ask the child to get on their hands and knees, blow the fish and crawl after it across the room. This is really fun!
- Place pieces of paper or "stepping stones" in a straight line. Ask your child to step onto the first "stone" with their <u>right</u> foot, then step onto the next "stone" with their <u>left</u> foot and hop. Ask your child to repeat this and step <u>starting with the left</u> foot. The action is right-step-hop, left-step-hop.

What will I see if I do all these things?

If you follow the suggestions regularly and repeatedly, your child's coordination will improve. Their limbs will be better coordinated and this will help them to ride a bike more easily.

Parent support activities (PSA)

What will I do if I don't see an improvement?

Ask yourself these questions:

- Have I been clear about what I expect from my child?
- Have I explained everything clearly?
- Am I doing this at least once a day with my child?
- Have I spotted signs of other gross or fine motor coordination difficulties, e.g. holding a pencil, picking up tiny objects, dressing, jumping, hopping, etc.?

What else could I do?

- If you are concerned about your child's movement or coordination, then perhaps consider a referral to an occupational therapist via your GP, health visitor or school.
- Discuss your concerns with your child's key worker at nursery or teacher at school.

PSA 10 Excessive salivation

What am I seeing?

My child dribbles a lot.

What do I want to make better?

To stop or reduce the dribbling.

What things do I need?

- Paper fish
- Large tray
- Straws
- Ping pong balls
- Goals
- Gummed paper
- Honey
- Mirror

What could I try?

Daily activities to help to tighten muscles in the mouth in order to reduce/stop dribbling.
   If your child uses a dummy, reduce the use gradually until they no longer need it (dummies can affect speech production and stimulate saliva).
   Play the following games every day:

- <u>Blowfish</u>. Cut out paper fish to blow along the floor.
- <u>Blow football</u>. Place a small goal at opposite ends of a large tray. Blow a ping pong ball from one side to the other to try to score a goal.
- <u>Blow painting</u>.
- <u>Blowing bubbles</u>.
- <u>Suck it up</u>. Give your child a drinking straw and ask them to transfer a paper shape from one place to another.
- <u>Lick and stick</u>. Make a picture or paper chain with gummed paper. Lots of licking!
- <u>Doughnut challenge</u>. Lick the sugar from a doughnut before eating it (**not** a daily activity).
- <u>Honey lips</u>. Spread honey on your child's lips and ask them to lick them clean.
- <u>Cheeky cheeks</u>. Ask your child to blow out their cheeks. Show them how to move the air from side to side.
- <u>Funny face</u>. Ask your child to pull a funny face whilst looking in a mirror and hold it for 5 to ten seconds.

What will I see if I do all these things?

Muscles in the face and mouth will begin to tighten and dribbling will reduce.

Parent support activities (PSA)

What will I do if I don't see an improvement?

Ask yourself these questions:

- Have I shown my child what to do correctly?
- Have I removed my child's dummy?
- Have I explained everything clearly?
- Am I doing this at least once a day with my child?

What else could I do?

- If you are still worried about your child's dribbling, then perhaps consider a referral to a speech therapist or occupational therapist via your GP, health visitor or school.
- Discuss your concerns with your child's key worker at nursery or teacher at school.

PSA 11 Toilet training

Parents and carers have a key role to play in effective toilet training. You may feel anxious and responsible when your child has not yet achieved this developmental stage. It is important to feel confident in trying to toilet train your child but try to avoid putting too much pressure on them. Toilet training can be achieved in a week or so if done consistently and confidently but the process requires patience!

Never return the child to nappies once you have made the decision! You must resist the temptation to put them back in a nappy for convenience once you have removed them.

Prepare

- From eighteen months onwards children may be ready to start toilet training. Visible signs of readiness may include less frequent soiling of nappies, coming at regular intervals.
- Talk about it first before introducing a potty. Get the child on board and get them involved with choosing a potty, knickers/pants, etc.
- Introduce the potty: one that sits on the floor is less scary than one that sits on the toilet. Your child can rest their feet on the floor and will feel more secure.
- Put the potty in their play area.
- Let your child sit on it whenever they like.

Teach

- Each time your child has a poo in the nappy, get them to help you put it into the potty.
- Explain to your child that this is where wee and poo belong instead of in the nappy.
- Encourage your child to sit on the potty with their clothes on or off.
- Look for signs that your child needs a wee or poo, e.g. some children will grunt or grimace, hide or give a little shudder. Always ask if they need the potty if you see it.
- Ask your child to sit on the potty regularly and praise/reward if they wee or poo.
- Talk to your child about where wee and poo goes and praise/reward them often. There are story books to help.
- When you think your child is ready make the decision to take your child out of nappies but stick to the decision.
- Be consistent!
- Nappies are sometimes needed for a little longer at night but once a toilet routine has been established you will find that they will usually become dry at night.
- Be sure to offer your child their last drink early in the evening and visit the toilet before bedtime.

Parent support activities (PSA)

School or nursery

- Clothes must be easy for the child to pull up and down independently. Wherever possible it is better to train the child with appropriate clothing rather than continuing to rely on the nappy or training pants.
- Make sure that a member of staff is given the responsibility of taking your child to the toilet at fixed, appropriate intervals throughout the morning/day.

Important note

It is not the responsibility of the nursery or school to toilet train your child. However, a nursery or school cannot refuse admission or to support you in toilet training your child and must not ask you to come in to change your child.

PSA 12 *Getting dressed*

All children must be given the best opportunity for successfully developing personal skills. We must **"Support the development of independent skills, particularly for children who are highly dependent upon adult support for personal care"**.

Dressing involves very coordinated small movements that some children may struggle with. It is likely most children will achieve these skills but some may not have acquired them in time for going to nursery or school. It is at this time when you may feel anxious about your child if they cannot dress independently.

How to help

There is always a temptation to dress your child, brush their teeth for them and put their coat and shoes on because it's quicker and you are in a hurry. Try to **avoid** doing this. Begin your day earlier to allow time for your child to try the dressing independently. Children need to practice every day to remember the movements required for dressing.
START WITH BIG MOVEMENTS . . . WORK TOWARDS SMALL.

Putting on a coat or shirt

Some children may find it difficult even to put one arm in one sleeve. In order to develop the small, coordinated movements required for putting on a coat try the following:

- Provide some small, coloured plastic hoops or Quoits, similar to those you throw at pegs on the ground (about 7/8cm in diameter).
- Ask your child to put their arm through each hoop one at a time and pull them right to the top of their arm. They could count the hoops or name the colours as they go, making it a bit more fun.
- They are threading their arm through the plastic hoop, mirroring the movement required to put one arm in one sleeve.
- Do this with both arms, starting with the arm they naturally use first. Practice this daily for several days.
- Next, ask your child to put one hoop on their arm then hold another hoop to the side of their shoulder and ask them to put their arm through the hoop from the side and pull it up to their shoulder. Repeat as often as possible.
- Next hold the second hoop behind the child's shoulder and ask them to put their arm in the hoop that is behind them. This involves a little twist of the body. You may have to show your child what to do.
- Practice this as often as possible.
- Next ask your child to put one arm in one sleeve of a large garment, e.g. an adult's shirt or coat, and encourage them to put their second arm in the second sleeve as you have shown them. Practice these movements until you think your child is ready to try with their own coat or shirt. Provide your child with dressing-up clothes, which are often bigger and easier to get on.
- Make getting dressed into a game. Have their clothes out ready for them to put on.

Your child needs to over-practice dressing. They need to memorise the small, coordinated movements needed to do this. It will help them to be able to dress independently.

PERSONAL, SOCIAL and EMOTIONAL

PSA 13 Difficulty sharing and taking turns

What am I seeing?

My child is unable or unwilling to share or take turns with other children. They get upset when having to take turns and then sometimes refuse to take part in the game or activity.

What do I want to make better?

I want my child to be able to take turns and share toys or play games without getting upset.

What things do I need?

You will need some tabletop games or building bricks.
  Rewards, such as "fun" stickers or other extra treat.

What could I try?

- Find out what it is that your child doesn't like to share or allow anyone else from having a turn.
- Sit with your child with an activity that you know your child likes or has chosen themselves. It must be an activity or game that requires turn-taking.
- If there are other children close by, make sure they are moved away. If there is another adult close by, ask them to take other children somewhere else.
- Begin the game/activity. You lead the game and begin first. Use language appropriate for the game, e.g. "It's my turn" or "I'll go first". Take your turn then say to your child that it's now their turn.
- During the game, model the language of turn taking, e.g. "Whose turn/go is it now?" or "It's your turn after me", or "You must wait until I've had my turn".
- Repeat this every day and gradually include more people, e.g. dad, mum, brother, sister, grandma, etc. Your child will be expected to wait longer for their turn.
- Reward your child for good turn taking. Reinforce by saying things like, "Good sharing". "Kind hands", etc.
- It may be worth asking your child how their behaviour makes other children feel— happy, sad, etc.

What will I see if I do all these things?

If you follow the suggestions regularly and repeatedly, your child will begin to cooperate and take turns with their friends and help to improve sharing with others.

What will I do if I don't see an improvement?

Ask yourself these questions:

- Have I been clear about what taking turns means and what I expect?
- Am I choosing activities that interest my child?

What else could I do?

- Teach the language your child needs for good sharing.
- Discuss your concerns with your child's key worker at nursery or teacher at school.

PSA 14 Aggressive behaviour

What am I seeing?

My child shows little control of their own behaviour. They cannot cope with conflict or confrontation, particularly when sharing or turn-taking is required. They can become very aggressive and often hurt other children, e.g. hitting, biting, hair pulling. They run away when confronted and scream and shout.

What do I want to make better?

- To stop my child from hitting or being physically aggressive to other children.
- To help my child manage their aggression and to do the right thing in conflict situations with other children.

What things do I need?

- You will need some positive rewards.
- Small jar with large pasta shapes.

What could I try?

- Approach your child calmly. Intervene quickly and firmly to protect the other child.
- Firmly tell your child to stop doing whatever they are doing to the other child, e.g. say your child's name and say, "Stop hitting", "Stop shouting", etc. Use hand gestures if necessary to reinforce your words.
- Make sure the other child is moved away. If there is another adult close by ask them to take the other child somewhere else.
- When your child has stopped being aggressive, take them away from the situation. Continue to reinforce "No hitting", "No biting", etc. Use very clear, simple language and/or gestures.
- Don't insist at this stage that your child apologises to the other child as this may upset the other child even more by bringing your child back. *You* could apologise for your child's behaviour. You may want them to apologise later when they are really sorry and want to make up with their friend/playmate.
- Reinforce what you expect when your child is playing with other children and in particular stress that they must not hit, bite, etc.
- Reward your child every time for doing the right thing. Start a collection of something your child likes and work towards a treat. Ask your child to add a pasta shape to the jar and give them a big reward when the jar is full.
- Don't wait for your child to do the wrong thing. Catch them "being good". Always try to be as positive as you can.

What will I see if I do all these things?

If you follow the suggestions regularly and repeatedly, your child will begin to do the right thing. They will learn that hitting and biting is not the right thing to do. They will begin to demonstrate an understanding of what is acceptable and unacceptable.

Parent support activities (PSA) 95

What will I do if I don't see an improvement?

Ask yourself these questions:

- Have I been clear about what I expect from my child?
- Have I asked everyone in the household to do the same as me if they see this behaviour?
- Am I certain that my child understands what I have said? How do I know this?
- Can my child communicate well using words rather than being physical.

What else could I do?

- Help my child to take turns and share. Teach them how to ask for things appropriately. Play games to role model what you mean.
- Have your child's hearing checked.**
- Have your child's speech and language skills checked out by referring to a speech and language therapist, if you have any concerns about this.
- Discuss your concerns with your child's key worker at nursery or teacher at school.

**Always rule out any hearing difficulties. This may be a contributing factor to unacceptable behaviour and/or speech delay.

PSA 15 *Finding it hard to make choices*

What am I seeing?

My child finds it difficult to make choices. They can never seem to decide what to do.

What do I want to make better?

I would like my child to be able to decide what to play with without an adult having to choose for them.

What things do I need?

- A piece of string/cord about one metre long (timeline/planner).
- A shoe box with a slit cut into the lid, perhaps decorated with colourful wrapping paper.
- Several pieces of blank paper or card, big enough to draw a simple picture or a set of photographs of toys or activities in the house (your child's school or nursery will be able to provide you with a selection of activity and object cards).
- Blu Tack® and a number of clothes pegs (one of which is decorated or made to look special in some way).

What could I try?

- To start with, instead of saying to your child, "What would you like to do?", say, "Would you like to . . . (something specific), or (something else specific)?" Then give them only two choices. For more choices, use a timeline.
- Attach the string/cord horizontally to a suitable wall or door using the Blu Tack®.
- Ask your child which of their favourite toys/games they would like to play with or activities they would like to do. Prepare or draw a picture of each of the things/activities they are interested in.
- Ask them to peg the three pictures onto the timeline/planner (starting from the left).
- Ask your child to look at the planner and choose where they want to play or what they want to do.
- Your child can then do the activity or play with the toy.
- When they have finished, encourage them to take the picture card off the timeline/planner and post it in the posting box.
- Ask your child to look at the second picture and do that activity or play with the toy.
- When your child understands how to use a timeline/planner, you can offer them the choice of more toys/activities.
- Always remind your child to remove the card/picture when they have finished.
- Keep doing this until your child uses the planner and makes choices independently.
- Always do the things you say you are going to do and at the time you have told your child if you want your child to do the right thing.

Parent support activities (PSA)

What will I see if I do all these things?

If you follow the suggested strategies every day your child will soon be able to make choices independently and confidently.

What will I do if I don't see an improvement?

Ask yourself these questions:

- Have I been clear about what I expect from my child?
- Does my child understand about the planning boards?
- Am I certain that my child understands what I have said? How do I know this?
- Am I offering interesting activities and/or toys?

What else could I do?

- Talk to your child's nursery or school about your concerns.

PSA 16 *Not doing as they are asked*

What am I seeing?

- My child is not doing as they are asked.
- Behaving differently to others, e.g. not sitting at the table with others.
- Pushing the boundaries, getting angry when asked to stop or change.
- Being unkind to others.

What do I want to make better?

To help my child do the right thing when asked.

What things do I need?

- A piece of string/cord about one metre long with some Blu Tack® and several clothes pegs—one peg should be different or special.
- You need some pictures or photos (you could draw them onto pieces of blank paper or card or use pictures that can be provided by your child's nursery or reception teacher) of things you want your child to do when asked, e.g. toys in the correct place, bath time, teatime, your child in pyjamas, etc.
- Sand timers and collectable rewards, e.g. coins, stickers, counters, reward charts, etc.

What could I try?

- Make sure your child is looking at you before speaking. Say very clearly and simply what you want your child to do.
- Instead of "*will you . . .*" or "*I would like you to . . .*", say, "*It's time to . . .*" or "*It's time for . . .*".
- Attach the string/cord to a suitable wall or door using the Blu Tack®. This is your timeline. Make a "picture story" of what will happen during the day by pegging pictures from left to right on your timeline. Clip the "special" peg to the first picture as you begin that activity. As you go from one activity to the next, move the special peg along to the next picture to show your progress during the day.
- Make sure your child knows what will be happening during the day, where they will be going and who they will be seeing.
- Try to avoid a cluttered room—tidy as you go along so that there is not too much to tidy all at once. Help your child to put one toy away before getting another one out.
- Try using a one-, two- or three-minute timer before asking your child to stop playing or do something different. Say, "*When the timer runs out it will be time to . . .*" and show a picture of the next activity. This is ideal for bath time or bedtime. Children need to have time to end their play before moving on.
- Reward your child every time for doing the right thing. Start a collection of something your child likes and work towards a treat.
- Always do the things you say you are going to do and at the time you have told your child if you want your child to do the right thing.

What will I see if I do all these things?

If you follow the suggestions regularly and repeatedly, your child will begin to do the right thing automatically. They will trust you and feel more confident and will be more willing to follow your instructions.

What will I do if I don't see an improvement?

Ask yourself these questions:

- Have I been clear about what I expect from my child?
- Have I asked everyone to do the same as me?
- Am I certain that my child understands what I have said? How do I know this? Has my child heard me?
- Am I allowing enough time for my child to do the right thing?

What else could I do?

- Have your child's hearing checked.
- Have your child's understanding checked out by referring to a speech and language therapist.
- Share what you have done with your child's nursery or school.

Index

2014 SEND Code of Practice 2

ability to construct and say simple sentences, activity for developing 23
ability to sit still, activity to improve 30
ability to use knife, fork and spoon, activity to develop 44
activity "action" cards strategy 23
age appropriate expressive language, activity for developing 19
aggressive behaviour, PSA for reducing 94–5
attention: checklist for 5; early years intervention activities for 27–32; PSA for difficulty with 73–4

balance and stability, activity to improve 35–7
behaviour of children: activity to modify 52; changes in 2; checklist for managing 6, 17; early years intervention activities for managing 59–62; identification and removal of barrier to improving 4; issues in 63
bilateral integration, activity for 39
bumping, PSA for reducing 79–80

card user guide, PSA for 67–8
checklist of observed behaviours 8; communication and language 8, 12–14; intervention activities 9–10; intervention record sheet 10–11; personal, social and emotional development 8, 16–17; physical development 8, 15–17
children: behavioural issues of 63; "catch up" period of 63; differences in behaviour in early stage 1; early identification and intervention of 1–3, 63; holistic profile creation for 4–7; making observations for 4

clarity of sounds and words, activity for developing 21
clear speaking, PSA for difficulty to 71–2
concentration, activity to improve 29
conductive hearing loss 20
confidence in talking, activity to improve 22, 56
confident and independent communication, activity to support 33–4
conversational skills, activity to improve 31
core strengthening, activity for 40
cutting, PSA for difficulty with 83–4

early years intervention activities: communication and language 18–34; personal, social and emotional development 47–62; physical development 35–46
Early Years Intervention Toolkit 8; checklist of observed behaviours 8–11; Intervention Record Sheet 8
excessive salivation, PSA for 87–8
expression: checklist of observed behaviour for 13; early years intervention activities for 23–6

facial and tongue muscles, activity to strengthen 46
falling, PSA for reducing 79–80
feelings: checklist for managing 17; early years intervention activities for managing 59–62
finding it hard to make choices, PSA for 96–7
fine motor coordination, activity to develop 42–3
Foundation Stage curriculum 63

Index

getting dressed, PSA for 91
"Going to Holland" analogy 64–5
gross movements, activity to slow 35–7

health of children: checklist of observed behaviour for 16; early years intervention activities for 44–6; and PSA 67, 79
holding pencil, PSA for difficulty to 81–2
holistic profile: checklist 5–6; creation for children 4, 7

ideas and sentences in conversation, activity for extending 26
inability to sit still, PSA for 75–6
independent choices, activity to make 57
independently put coat or shirt on, activity for child to 45
interest in other activities and resources, activity to begin to show 58
Intervention Record Sheet 10–11
interventions: activities 9–10; for children 2–3

Key Stage One curriculum 63
Key Stage Two curriculum 63

limited speech, PSA for 69–70
listening: checklist for 5; early years intervention activities for 27–32; PSA for difficulty with 73–4

make eye contact and listen, activity to support 27
memory skills, checklist for 5
motor skills and movement, checklist for 6
moving and handling of children: checklist of observed behaviour for 15; early years intervention activities for 35–43
muscle exercise 21

not doing as they are asked, PSA for 98–9
not understanding or responding to adults, PSA for 77–8

parallel play, activity to engage in 47
parents: "Going to Holland" analogy for 64–5; as partners 63; practitioners approaching to 63–4; activity for child to separation with increasing confidence 54
Parent Support Activities (PSA) 65–6; aggressive behaviour 94–5; attention and listening, difficulty with 73–4; card user guide 67–8; clear speaking, difficulty to 71–2; cutting, difficulty with 83–4; excessive salivation 87–8; finding it hard to make choices 96–7; getting dressed 91; holding pencil, difficulty to 81–2; inability to sit still 75–6; limited speech 69–70; not doing as they are asked 98–9; not understanding or responding to adults 77–8; Parental Support Activity Sheets (PSAs) 10; riding bike, difficulty to 85–6; sharing and taking turns, difficulty to 92–3; toilet training 89–90; tripping, falling and bumping 79–80
personal, social and emotional development 8, 16–17; aggressive behaviour 94–5; difficulty to sharing and taking turns 92–3; finding it hard to make choices 96–7; making relationships 16, 47–53; managing feelings and behaviour 17, 59–62; not doing as they are asked 98–9; PSA 67; self-confidence and self-awareness 17, 54–8
physical development 8, 15–16; cutting, difficulty with 83–4; excessive salivation 87–8; getting dressed 91; health and self care 44–6, 67, 79; holding pencil, difficulty to 81–2; moving and handling 35–43; PSA 67; riding bike, difficulty to 85–6; toilet training 89–90; tripping, falling and bumping 79–80
picture exchange concept 18
picture object snap game 21
planning and organisation, checklist for 6
practitioners 65; approaching parents 63–4; early identification of changes in children 4, 9, 63; Early Years Intervention Toolkit for 8; encouraging parents to use PSA 65–6; interact with children 2; providing intervention activities to children 9–10; role in supporting child children 2–3, 8

Index

pronunciation of sounds and words, activity for developing 20
PSA *see* Parent Support Activities (PSA)

relationships: checklist for making 16; early years intervention activities for making 47–53
respond appropriately to adults and children, activity to support to 60–1
respond appropriately to routines and expectations, activity to support to 59
respond to how other children are feeling, activity to 48
riding bike, PSA for difficulty to 85–6

self-awareness: checklist for observing 17; early years intervention activities for 54–8
self care: checklist of observed behaviour for 16; early years intervention activities for 44–6; and PSA 67, 79
self-confidence: checklist for observing 17; early years intervention activities for 54–8
sharing skills: activity to develop 51; PSA for difficulty to 92–3
single object picture cards 19
single-word vocabulary development, activity for 24
social interaction: activity to develop 32, 49, 55; checklist for 5
spatial awareness, activity for 38
speaking: checklist of observed behaviour for 12; early years intervention activities for 18–21
Special Educational Need 2

speech, language and communication 8; attention and listening, difficulty with 73–4; checklist for 5; clear speaking, difficulty to 71–2; expression 13, 23–6; inability to sit still 75–6; limited speech 69–70; listening and attention 27–32; not understanding or responding to adults 77–8; PSA 67; speaking 12, 18–21; supporting receptive 14, 33–4
strengths of children, holistic profile checklist for observing 6
supporting receptive language and communication: checklist of observed behaviours 14; through environment 33–4
supportive, inclusive teaching strategies, activity to develop 62

toilet training, PSA for 89–90
tripod pencil grip, activity to develop 41
tripping, PSA for reducing 79–80
turn taking skills: activity to develop 31, 50; PSA for difficulty to 92–3
two way non-verbal communication, activity for developing 18

understanding of children, checklist of observed behaviour for 14

waiting, activity to improve encouraging 31
word confusion, activity for reducing 25
word/picture cards 18